SURVIVING PAEDOPHILIA

traumatic stress after organised and network child sexual abuse

SURVIVING PAEDOPHILIA

traumatic stress after organised and network child sexual abuse

Kate Cairns

Qualcar author

Trentham Books

QUAKER AUTHOR

First published in 1999 by Trentham Books Limited

Trentham Books Limited
Westview House
734 London Road
Oakhill
Stoke on Trent
Staffordshire
England ST4 5NP

British Cataloguing in Publication Data
A catalogue record for this book is available from the British
Library
ISBN: 1 85856 136 1 (pb)
ISBN: 1 85856 135 3 (hb)

Designed and typeset by Trentham Print Design Ltd., Chester
and printed in Great Britain by The Cromwell Press Ltd., Wiltshire

Contents

Preface

Paedophilia is a frightening disease. It provokes unexpectedly virulent Lynch mobs both on our streets and in our television studios, it damages countless lives, many covertly, and has lately persuaded a generally liberal Home Secretary to traduce the very Human Rights we would most wish paedophiles to respect. Quite a catalogue for a single mental disease. In such a dire context, a book about *Surviving Paedophilia* comes as a breath of fresh air. There is lacerating realism here: the toxic damage, the chaos, the injuries to second, third, even fourth parties. And yet, running through the entire book is a steadfastness, a solid determination to confront the harsh realities of the wounds inflicted, coupled with an almost obsessive concern not to lose sight of the humanity that underlies even the most provocative of the child victim's destructivities. Amid such clarity of vision, optimism like this is infrequent and when you find it, as here, it is heart-warming.

Paedophilia is frightening in another way too. Not only does it corrode the foundation stones of its victims' personalities, so clearly described herein, it actually corrupts the very societies in which it flourishes; in Belgium, North Wales, Cleveland, the travails paedophilia inflicts are deep and terrible. During my study tour of Child Abuse Centres in the United States, I learnt of a Judges' Convention on Child Sex Abuse, where one judge was discovered molesting another judge's grand-daughter. Later a social worker in Ohio told me how she was visited late one night by the local mayor, who said that if she proceeded further with her investigations into paedophilia, he would guarantee she would never work in Ohio again. Only the other day in conversation at a friend's house, a visitor recounted how in a past job, her pre-viously friendly and supportive boss had told her, in menacing terms, that the case she was currently pursuing against a serial paedophile offender must be dropped. This is England, today. What sinister forces are induced by this disease? Calm reasoned debate of such an emotive issue is urgently required and happily this book gives us an excellent start.

What we need, as Kate Cairns makes clear, is a better understanding of paedophilia itself. The last time I described my approach to it, the psychiatric staff made life unpleasant for me. It is hard to change a lifetime of psychiatric training, but unless we do we shall continue to get nowhere with this insidious and malignant disease. Perhaps if I sketch out the way I see paedophilia developing, it will become obvious how closely this follows on from Kate Cairns' approach. Only with insight into its causes can we come anywhere nearer to wholly effective treatment.

One of the most tragic aspects of victims of paedophilia, which hits hardest those who try and comfort them, is that the children bring with them into their new home, elements of the destruction and dis-trust they learnt in the last. This is what is so soul-destroying for all the carers, as Kate Cairns makes graphically clear. The second, third and fourth level of carers are being punished, quite directly, for sins they have never committed, and would never wish to commit. The abused child cannot (at first) distinguish between abusive families and supportive families. It's like being born into a concentration camp: those with power can only be in league with the guards who, if you value your life, you never ever trust.

Talking to paedophiles about these deeper issues, it is clear to me that they too have been taught to see the world through distorting lenses. They too suffer from gross misperceptions, bizarrely misperceiving infants as sexually attractive and adults as not. Being now adult, they embroider their arguments with some ferocity. Yet the fact remains that adult to adult sexual contact is normal, and sex with infants is not. Freud's influence does not help. After his father died in 1896, Freud seriously lost his way, preferring to disappear into a dream world of symbolisms and fantasies – distortions that have set back the study of child abuse by 100 years. In April 1896, however, his acute clinical observation compelled him to coin the term 'pseudo-hereditary' to cover the point just made: how abusive distortions can be passed on from one family member to another, almost as if they were a type of social infection. In Freud's 1896 view, no one abuses children sexually unless they have been instructed, or learnt how to do it. These earliest experiences are the source of the intensity, the drive, the ferocity with which these deranged personalities grind up infants, poisoning their multiple families, their society, and sometimes their nation, in the process.

Thus there is a curious parallel between the deep and toxic roots of paedophilia and the anguishes of the abused child so heartrendingly described here. Trust in both contexts is at a premium, and so is courage. Without these invaluable resources, no progress can be made in breaking such toxic patterns. The best way to protect our children, and if pseudo-hereditary is right, to curtail future paedophilia, is to give them confidence that adults are here to help, that adults can become trustworthy. We need to find ways to empower these children and show them that there is a brighter future for them than the horrendous nightmare they have left behind. This is how I see Kate Cairns' message and an excellent message it is too. The way is thorny, arduous, uncertain, and often unclear but unless we act upon it, how can we save our children who are after all our future?

Dr Bob Johnson
Consultant Psychiatrist

Foreword

At first there was my own experience, the feeling, sensing, and thinking which has built up over years to become the story of my life so far, and which changes each day as I discover a little more of the adventure. This direct experience has itself expanded and changed through conversations with many people and through reading the ideas of wise and experienced others.

Conversations with several hundred people have informed my thoughts as I wrote this book. I have listened to children who have been victims of paedophile abuse, and to adults who were victims as children. I have listened to the parents and grandparents, brothers and sisters, partners and children of people who were victims as children. I have heard from, and listened to, colleagues from many disciplines and from various parts of Britain; foster carers, residential child care staff, police officers, social workers, teachers, nurses, doctors, child care consultants, child protection consultants, therapists, journalists, and academics have all shared ideas or talked to me about their experiences.

Many who have generously given time, or revived painful memories, did so trusting that I would never reveal any hint of their identity. Some for professional reasons cannot be identifiable. Others still live in deep, and probably realistic, fear of the perpetrators of abuse and those who protect the perpetrators. I hope that I have been able to say what needs to be said without breaking that trust. If I have not said it adequately, it is because I lack the skill and not because I lack the will to convey the essence of the stories I have heard.

These conversations are not a substitute for research. That still needs to be done. But I believe that we need to move towards new understandings of the effects of paedophilia before we will begin to generate social and medical research which addresses the real issues we all face and often call by other names. Until we know and accept that we have a problem, we cannot begin to address it sensibly. At the moment, we know clearly enough that there is a problem, but we seem to think that it is a problem which belongs to paedophiles and their victims. I hope to contribute to a point of view which says that the problem which we need to investigate and for which we need to discover solutions belongs to us all.

Traumatic stress in others touches deep roots in us. It challenges us to confront the forces of avoidance, denial and minimisation in ourselves. It requires every one of us to recognise and confront our own humanity and vulnerability. My understanding of this has grown over thirty years of social work, child care, and the teaching of child care before, after, and at times concurrently with, a continuous twenty two year period of living and working in our own home with a large family group of children. Most of these children had suffered severe childhood trauma before coming to live with us, and some had been victims of paedophilia.

We established this family group in 1975. From 1986 onwards, after eleven years of cheerful caring for and learning from the children, it was becoming clear that external support services in social work, child and family guidance, psychology, psychiatry and psychotherapy of all kinds were diminishing in availability and consequently in effectiveness. At the same time the needs of certain children in our care were drawing us ineluctably to discover the total life impact of the effects of paedophile abuse. By 1992 the impact on the family group in general, and on me in particular, of my inability to generate an appropriate service response for and on behalf of these children had become critical.

The next four years had the quality of a waking nightmare which I recognised then, and now more fully understand, to be the result of traumatic stress. It was salutary, indeed therapeutic, to discover that I was not alone, that colleagues shared many of my experiences. The extent, nature, and prevalence of the suffering which presented itself to me once I started to ask simple questions was, however, a source of profound concern.

Many of these colleagues are still suffering in silence, often an enforced silence. They may feel unable to tell their stories without breaking professional confidences, they may be afraid to tell their stories for fear of penalties which they perceive as dreadful, or they may have repeatedly tried to speak their truth already and been ignored or silenced. I have written this book for them, as well as for the children who hardly ever can tell us the full story of their suffering. I hope it helps.

Acknowledgements

I am deeply grateful to all the people who have talked to me about their experiences; also to those who were willing to see me, but time or money or both ran out before we met. Now that I have rather more free time, please give me a call and we can get together. I hope for all of you that I have managed to catch an image of the experience we have all shared in one way or another.

I have drawn heavily on the work of the thirty four people from seven countries whose writings on the subject have been gathered together by Bessel A. van der Kolk, Alexander C. McFarlane, and Lars Weisaeth and published as *Traumatic Stress: the effects of overwhelming experience on mind, body and society* (Guilford Press, 1996). Taken together with other literature on the subject, I have found this an invaluable source book and guide. I hope I have given an adequate and accurate account of the research and theories they put forward; any mistakes I have made are mine and not theirs.

Lil Brooks and Johnny Lovell were my supervisors; they kept me sane and I don't know what I would have done without them. My thanks to Brian and the family, who were there. I do know what I would have done without them, that's why I am grateful.

Guildenstern	I think I have it. A man talking sense to himself is no madder than a man talking nonsense not to himself.
Rosencrantz	Or just as mad.
Guildenstern	Or just as mad.
Rosencrantz	And he does both.
Guildenstern	So there you are.
Rosencrantz	Stark raving sane.

(*Rosencrantz and Guildenstern are Dead* by Tom Stoppard)

Chapter 1

First thoughts

There are things we learn because we want to, and things we learn because we must. There are also things we learn because we can no longer avoid knowing. Thirty years ago, I remember, we did not know that parents sometimes abuse and torture and kill their children. Then the 'battered baby syndrome' gained recognition, and we taught ourselves to look steadily at the horror and to intervene on behalf of the children. Such learning causes us distress. It is natural to resist it.

Once one barrier had fallen, others followed. Incest was another taboo subject. Gradually we came to understand that the taboo was effective in stopping us from thinking about it, and certainly effective in stopping us from talking about it, but unfortunately was not effective in stopping everyone from doing it. We learned that children were suffering because of this, that the pain it caused us to discover this truth and acknowledge it, though great, was trivial compared to the pain suffered by the victims of incest.

Thirty years is a very short time to learn so much. We now know that children do suffer physical and sexual abuse, and that these experiences harm them. We have resolved as a society to do something to protect children from such harm, and we have made laws to enable us to do so. We debate these matters openly, and the many voices raised and views expressed let us know that we are thinking, that learning is taking place.

I am a teacher learning interests me. So does not-learning, the energy we put into resisting new knowledge which will change us. When the next logical stage on this journey of discovery of the world of child-

1

hood suffering opened up in front of me, I resisted it. I had learned about the physical abuse of children, and had recognised that part of the difficulty around changing our attitudes was to do with the institutionalised acceptance that children could be assaulted with impunity, child beating being sanctioned by law and custom. I had accepted the reality of child sexual abuse, and understood that some families and some individuals made use of children as sexual objects. Yet when I was presented with evidence that the sexual abuse of children is also institutionalised in our society I resisted the learning.

That resistance seems to be widespread. It is deeply painful for us to recognise that, though not sanctioned by law, in parts of our society the sexual abuse of children is sanctioned by custom and belief. There are people who are respected and respectable who privately, and sometimes openly, believe that it is acceptable to use children as sexual objects. To recognise this, and to acknowledge that we do not know one another as we thought we did, that we have very little idea how any other person we meet thinks or behaves in the privacy of their sexuality and may, for all we know, be abusing children daily, hurts us profoundly.

I had to learn it at last because of the children. Once we realise that children who are victims of such abuse suffer so terribly that they can become disordered, and then go on to harm themselves and others, it becomes much more difficult to resist the learning. Once we have seen the scars, witnessed the distress, waited at the hospital to know whether the suicide attempt will be successful or whether the child will live to try again, it becomes much harder to close our eyes and stop our ears. And when children tell us they have been silenced, when they insist, with terror in their eyes, that if they ever say it they will die, then it becomes much easier for us to find a voice ourselves.

A word about the language I have chosen. I have elected to write about paedophilia because, so far as I can see, that is the terminology of the extremes of a debate which urgently needs to be moved onto the middle ground of openness and rationality. Bigots write about paedophilia as though it were an extreme and inhuman perversion such as necrophilia, and urge that extreme and inhuman vengeance be wrought upon paedophiles. Paedophiles write about paedophilia as though it were harmless, as though paedophiles love children in much the same way as oenophiles love wine, and urge that paedophilia should be accepted as one of the many diverse ways human beings may relate to one another sexually.

These attitudes miss the point. Paedophilia leads to behaviour which has effects. I have come to believe that the most significant effect of paedophilia is that it produces victims. The children, their families, those who care for them, and a range of professionals who become involved in working with the results of paedophilia, fall victim to the circles of harm which spread outward from paedophile behaviour.

Despite the title, I have generally avoided the language of survival. Instead I have chosen to write about victims and sufferers. Where in the text I have written of survivors, I mean those who have failed to die as a result of the horrors they have suffered, for I well know that not everyone does survive paedophilia. To speak of survival in any wider sense than this sheer physical failing to die, is to misrepresent the personal, social, and political forces which oppress and perpetually revictimize those who suffer harm as a result of the activities of paedophiles.

> Most victims who are conscious of the effects of trauma on their lives preserve their self-protective instincts and are highly ambivalent about having people find out what has happened to them. ...
>
> If memories of child abuse .... are not worked through, they tend to be expressed as irrational symptoms – behaviours that represent derivations of unresolved aspects of the trauma. ...
>
> Since both victims and bystanders experience intense emotions when confronted with these behaviours, they are likely to lose sight of the fact that they are rooted in past trauma. Instead, both will construct complex rationales to justify their reactions: elaborate grievances, in the case of the victims and diagnostic constructs that invariably come to have a pejorative meaning, in the case of the bystanders. These grievances and diagnoses are designed to return a sense of control to the parties involved; ironically, however, both are likely to perpetuate the trauma ... The trauma will thus continue to be played out between helpless supplicants/victims/caregivers and predators/manipulators/oppressors. Calling victims 'survivors' is a euphemism that denies the reality of these dichotomies of powerlessness (van der Kolk et al, 1996, pp31-33).

The title 'Surviving Paedophilia' thus becomes a statement of hope, a promise made to those who, in living out their lives with all the grace and courage possible to them, have given me a story to be told.

The 'Carer's Stories' are my own, written some years ago when I was recovering from post traumatic stress disorder, and trying to make sense of more than twenty years of looking after, and working with, children, some of whom had been victims of paedophile abuse. Originally written for training purposes all names in it, including mine, have been changed; I have kept this convention intact, for, in the words of L. P. Hartley (1955), 'the past is a foreign country; they do things differently there', and now I have a different story to tell. All the events, conversations and remarks in these stories actually happened, but the personalities and attributes of the children represented are composite and not identifiable. The twelve children involved are all now adult, and have been fully consulted about the use of this material. Most of the story entitled 'Fear' was published in *The Guardian* (1 May 1996) as an article on fostering children who have suffered multiple abuse.

I have chosen not to discuss in any detail what it is that paedophiles do to children. This book is an exploration of the effects of paedophilia on various groups of people, a consideration of the harm arising from the activities of paedophiles not a description of those activities. I shall argue that the harm done by paedophilia is so great that it constitutes trauma, and that it is the traumatic stress and the disorders which can arise from it which change and harm the victims for years after the physical damage and emotional, and sometimes physical, torture have ended. There is also lasting physical damage, of course. I have worked with children and adults whose bodies bear scars and deformities which almost certainly are the result of the physical injuries they suffered at the hands of paedophiles. After some years those things are virtually impossible to prove, and in any case the injuries are compounded by years of subsequent self-harm and lack of self-care.

There is then a delicate balance to be struck. To avoid activating the voyeurism which can afflict any one of us as we try to grasp what goes on behind closed doors, yet also to avoid clinical coldness as we venture into territory which above all must be a place where we and the victims and the perpetrators all retain the humanity we share.

The activities of paedophiles are very varied. For a collection of papers outlining elements of the debates around organised abuse see *Organised Abuse: the current debate* (Bibby, 1996); the views presented are appropriately varied, the issues raised are important. Among the papers included in *Organised Abuse* are descriptions of, or pointers to, all of the following patterns associated with paedophilia. Organised sexual abuse may be seen as family patterns organised around sexual abuse, individuals organising patterns of sexual abuse across time, and groups of individuals organising networks to abuse children or to share pornography or information relating to the sexual abuse of children.

Paedophile activities include organised patterns of incest in single families or groups of families, which may involve multigenerational sexual activity of all kinds, the use of pornographic material within the family or network of families, the production of home-made pornographic material, and perhaps the exchange of money or goods for children or for child pornography. Children may be sold for food, or to pay debts, or to make extra money for the family. The children are likely to be physically abused and are certain to be emotionally abused as well as suffering sexual abuse.

Lone paedophiles, with or without a history of incest in their own family, may organise their lives around a career of paedophilia; they may seek work which provides access to children, especially vulnerable children; they may make opportunities to gain the trust of families, as lodger, family friend, teacher, baby sitter, sports coach, or partner to a single parent; they may establish a role with unprotected groups of children by targeting churches or youth groups, or by setting up 'projects' to meet a community need. The sexual activity will depend upon the tastes of the abuser. It may involve children of the same gender as the abuser, of the opposite gender, or be indiscriminate; it may focus on children of a particular age range, or with a particular disability; it may involve a single child, or groups of children. Children may be bribed, coerced, threatened, seduced, drugged, or tortured to ensure compliance and silence. Children may be used to recruit others.

There is also institutional paedophile abuse, in which paedophiles take over the running of institutions for vulnerable children, and establish regimes in which the sexual abuse of children is the central organising principle. These can be very carefully constructed, planned and put together with great patience and intelligence, or relatively haphazard and opportunistic. The latter are more likely to be detected, but either way great numbers of the most vulnerable children in our society may be abused over many years in such institutional care. The second Utting Report, *People Like Us* (1997), raises many issues about the safety of children in institutional care and foster care.

Finally there are the many forms of organised crime which depend upon, or have links with, paedophilia. These include local, national, and international networks of male and female child prostitution, child pornography, and the trade in information on access to vulnerable children. There are links to the drugs trade and to the adult sex industry. Organised paedophile rings and networks include people from all walks of life, including some people who have great power and influence. This creates a link between organised serious crime and the central structures of our society. Wherever there is an interface between organised crime and social and political power, corruption flourishes.

Like blast from a bomb, circles of harm spread outward from paedophilia, making victims of any who stand in its way. At the centre are the children, the primary victims who will bear the scars forever. Then there are those closest to them − whoever loves them enough to feel the wounds and suffer harm because of them − secondary victims through loving those who suffer most. Further from the centre are those whose work requires them to immerse themselves in the world of paedophilia − professionals it is true, but not prepared by training or experience for what they may uncover; and there are tertiary victims here, searching for a language to express what they have learned and an audience to hear it. And beyond is the whole social order, for where there is corruption, no part of the social fabric can escape the taint.

Chapter 2
Childhood Trauma
the fragmenting self

What is trauma?

In March 1987 the Herald of Free Enterprise ferry foundered disastrously. Some work I was asked to do after that disaster led me to read extensively about the phenomena of trauma, traumatic stress, and post traumatic stress disorder. At that time the literature was relatively sparse; in the years since the Herald disaster there has been a huge development in the study of trauma, and many books and articles are now available as a result of that study.

This is a very specific and specialist use of the word *trauma*. In Greek the word means wound, and in general medical use it is used to denote physical wounds. From the very origins of psychiatry more than a hundred years ago trauma was being associated with the profound emotional and behavioural disturbances of hysteria. In this sense trauma seems to have been regarded as a psychic wound resulting from an event so horrifying that the individual affected is unable to assimilate it into normal conscious awareness.

It was this work on the genesis and maintenance of hysterical disorders undertaken in the late nineteenth century by such eminent medical men as Charcot, Janet and Freud which led Janet to coin the word 'subconscious' to describe memories and mental schemes which are outside conscious awareness, a concept which was to become central to the work of Freud in developing psychoanalytic theory (van der Kolk, Weisaeth and van der Hart, in van der Kolk *et al*, 1996, pp 52-56).

Yet more than a hundred years later a major textbook of psychology for A-level students, undergraduates and nurses has no reference to trauma in its nine hundred pages, no reference to traumatic stress and only one fleeting reference to post traumatic stress disorder (Gross, 1996). The extraordinary silence on the subject of trauma in so many standard texts is an indicator of an intrinsic difficulty which needs to be raised early and remembered constantly. Physical wounds can be seen, or at least detected, as real material alterations in the state of an organism. Psychic wounds, however, are always invisible and in day to day encounters can be detected only by way of the changes they produce in the physiology, feelings and behaviour of the victim. Such alterations in the way a person functions could be explained in many ways.

There are four factors which may be identified as significant in exploring the denial of the importance of trauma in our society. First there is the history of the study of trauma. Originally Freud was working along the same lines as Charcot and Janet in considering that trauma was at the root of hysteria (van der Kolk, Weisaeth and van der Hart in van der Kolk *et al*, 1996, p54) but as his work progressed he became convinced that the repression of unacceptable desires, rather than the intrusion and avoidance of unintegrated memories, was the most important cause of hysteria. Although he never entirely lost sight of the impact of traumatic memories on individual suffering, he never established a unified theory, but instead developed two separate models for the generation of neurosis. The developing discipline of psychiatry became preoccupied with the psychoanalytic model of neurosis as the product of defence mechanisms generated as an intrapsychic response to unacceptable impulses, and trauma came to be seen as generally irrelevant to the practice of psychiatry.

Trauma as a direct cause of disabling feelings and destructive behaviour has also been politically unacceptable for most of the period in which the knowledge base was available to develop an integrated theory of traumatic stress. Our political and legal structures depend largely on the concept of individuals being responsible for their own prosocial and antisocial behaviour, a concept which is not lost in a developed theory of trauma, but is certainly changed in ways which would radically affect our political life if understood and incorporated.

Dr. Bob Johnson was the psychiatrist at the centre of controversy when he resigned from his post at Parkhurst Prison after the special unit in which he worked was closed to category A prisoners, despite the demonstrable success of his work with these most violent prisoners. Johnson maintains that his treatment by the then Home Secretary Michael Howard and the subsequent attempts to destroy his medical records were a direct political response to the threat which his methods posed to established theories and practice in the treatment of crime (*The Guardian*, 27 January 1996). His methods are built on the premise that extreme violence arises out of childhood trauma, and that treatment which focuses on resolving and integrating the trauma will reduce the violent behaviour and produce self-control.

Living with and within an adversarial legal system further complicates the political issues around the acceptance of a theory of trauma. Under this sort of system, if an individual is suffering a disabling condition they may be cared for and have their needs met by society on humanitarian grounds. If, however, they can demonstrate and prove that some other individual or responsible body was responsible (in the sense of to blame) for their suffering, then they acquire a different legal status and may be eligible for compensation.

This naturally has an effect upon the political acceptability of trauma theory; imagine the implications for such an adversarial social order if war veterans or fire-fighters were able to claim compensation for the disabling effects of the work society asked them to do. With the rise in interest in traumatic stress in recent years, these issues are even now being fought out in protracted legal battles in our courts.

A third factor affecting the invisibility of trauma and its victims in our society has to do with the social structures which make up that society. Despite the famous or infamous pronouncement of Margaret Thatcher (then Prime Minister of the UK) that 'there is no such thing as society', our everyday reality is that we live as part of social structures. Human beings everywhere are found in groups, and those groups always develop some sort of structure. Those structures are built on our capacity and need to form social relationships with others. Victims of trauma, especially victims of trauma perpetrated upon them by others, ultimately pose a threat to the social order. Trauma, as we shall see, leads to the breakdown of fundamental beliefs and assumptions about the world, such as the belief that the world is essentially just or benevolent, that people have control over their lives, or that bad things do not ultimately happen to good people. The structures of society are built upon such beliefs. Trauma victims, if fully acknowledged and heard, challenge the most basic assumptions of our social order. 'Victims are the members of society whose problems represent the memory of suffering, rage, and pain in a world that longs to forget.' (van der Kolk and McFarlane in van der Kolk *et al*, 1996, p28).

Finally, there is a personal and individual tendency to deny the existence or potency of trauma. This is where we are at real risk of disappearing into our own circularity, yet it is an issue which must be faced if we are ever to examine fairly and justly the question of, and questions raised by, childhood trauma. Trauma exists; we may acknowledge that its existence has been denied or minimised in history, we may recognise the convoluted arguments and negations by which it has been denied a political existence, we may understand and even feel the mechanisms by which social groups defend themselves (ourselves) against the pain and disruption of trauma, and yet we may still find ourselves at a personal level denying the reality of trauma.

There are two strands to this individual denial of reality. One, the more straightforward to deal with, arises out of empathy. The suffering which can follow traumatic stress is intense and as transmissible at the level of feelings as it is incommunicable in words; therapists in this area will know all too well how powerfully the phenomenon of counter transference operates in trauma work. Trauma victims can generate defensive, self-protective reactions in others without ever saying a word about their plight. Thus their suffering is denied before it is ever uttered.

The second component of this denial springs from our own unacknowledged and unintegrated trauma. The facts and figures of trauma research make it clear that many people experience trauma which they cannot remember, the management of which at an unconscious level determines a whole range of patterned reactions and personality traits. Alice Miller was right; the truth we could not tell ourselves as children for fear of annihilation becomes the uncrossable limit of our thought processes as adults (Miller, 1992, pp129ff). By its nature trauma hides itself behind deep defences. If someone who suffered trauma as a child is living successfully as an adult, then either they have worked through and integrated the trauma, or they have developed highly successful and impenetrable psychic defences which encapsulate the trauma and shield the survivor from disabling pain.

These defences, insofar as they exist in your psyche or mine, prevent us from recognising, or even seeing, anything which would remind us of the trauma we suffered and which therefore would summon into consciousness the long and successfully buried pain. So long as these defences operate, we can live next door to, or work with, or even live with, victims of trauma and yet their pain will be invisible to us.

Denial is very, very difficult to hold steady in our vision. After all, your denial is obvious to me, while mine does not exist. Some years ago I was asked to accompany someone to a meeting of Alcoholics Anonymous. There I met two colleagues. I think that they were there because they have a dependency on alcohol, they think that I was there because I have a dependency on alcohol. All of us know that denial is at the heart of problems with the misuse of alcohol. Now, whenever I meet those colleagues in a social setting I am in a situation which I can only accept with good humour, but can never realistically resolve. The phenomenon of denial has me in its grasp. They think that they know that I have a problem which I am likely sometimes or often to deny because that is the nature of the problem, so the more I deny that I have a problem ...

Yet it is clear that the reality of trauma as a powerful force in the lives of individuals and groups and whole societies has been denied historically, politically, socially and personally throughout the whole time when parallel developments in philosophy, psychology and the relevant biological sciences would have made this a likely candidate for study. Throughout that time a few voices have always been raised, pointing out the processes of the remembering and forgetting of extreme suffering and extreme fear which so dramatically shape our lives; and art and music and literature have always explored the nature and process of human suffering in the face of natural, social or personal disaster.

In recent years, the study of trauma began with examining the effects of natural disasters such as bush fires in Australia and disasters arising from human errors or negligence such as the Bradford fire disaster or the loss of the Herald of Free Enterprise. One of the things that first struck me as I began to study trauma and traumatic stress arising from disasters was the apparent relationship between the long term effects of traumatic stress suffered by some victims of disaster, and the day to day experience of the children with whom I had been living and working for many years. At that time the relationship between certain kinds of experience in childhood and post traumatic stress disorder was neither established nor accepted. It remains controversial, and is a field requiring further research.

Yet the more that the subject is studied, the more that links are being made between the effects of trauma as a result of disaster and the effects of childhood trauma. Which may be a return to some first thoughts, for in 1896 Freud suggested that 'a precocious experience of sexual relations ... resulting from sexual abuse committed by another person ... is the specific cause of hysteria ... not merely (as Charcot had claimed) an agent provocateur' (Freud, 1896 quoted in van der Kolk *et al*, p54).

Trauma is real. It is the wound we sustain when we are exposed to experience so horrifying that it overwhelms our capacity to process the experience. It leads to the physiological and psychological response we call traumatic stress.

What is traumatic stress?
Confronted with experience too horrifying to be assimilated, the brain has mechanisms which provide the greatest possible chance that the human organism will survive. In a situation of trauma these mechanisms are activated automatically in parts of the brain generally regarded as primitive in terms of human evolution. They are, we may guess, the legacy to us all of our ancient ancestors who did not get eaten by sabre tooth tigers.

The sequence goes something like this. Sensory stimuli, activating the central nervous system by way of the sense organs, generate activity in the thalamus, an area of the brain which acts to convert incoming stimuli into signals which can be accepted and interpreted in other areas of the brain. Recent research (see van der Kolk *et al*, 1996, chapter twelve and particularly pp 293 – 294) suggests that the signal leaving the thalamus is split. The main part of the signal travels to the pre-frontal cortex, the most recent areas of the brain in evolutionary terms, for recognition and integration, but a fragment of the signal travels to the amygdala, part of the much more primitive limbic system.

The amygdala normally functions as an area of the brain which allows us to attribute emotional significance to our experience. Thus when sensory information arrives at the pre-frontal cortex, this will in turn be transmitted to the amygdala for emotional colouring to be added to enable accurate appraisal of the incoming data. The amygdala transforms the sensory signals into physiological changes which initiate and control emotional response.

The sensory input from the thalamus arrives at the amygdala earlier than that transmitted from the pre-frontal cortex (Carter, 1998, p94). This priming of the amygdala, which promotes survival in a potentially dangerous environment, indicates that emotional evaluation precedes conscious processing. Our brain function is such that we always respond emotionally before we are able to respond rationally.

In situations of extreme perceived threat the response of the amygdala is also extreme and very rapid. The autonomic nervous system response to trauma will be activated before it is possible for the individual to make any conscious appraisal of the event which has provoked that reaction.

Confronted with a situation likely to provoke severe distress, the triggering of the amygdala causes the body to flood with stress hormones, priming the body for fight or flight, and self-generated pain-killers, since threat can lead to injury, injury can lead to pain, and pain can disable us from being able to fight back or run away. These stress hormones, in turn, have the effect of turning off areas of the brain whose functioning might slow us up. Specifically, activity in both the hippocampus and Broca's area reduce significantly; the hippocampus normally functions to create a cognitive map for the emotional responses generated from the amygdala, that is it allows us to put words to feelings, and Broca's area has a major function in the creation and integration of language as speech and narrative memory.

Thus at the point of trauma there are no words for what is happening to us because the areas of our brains which generate the words are turned off. Trauma is always wordless terror.

It is the combination of the event, the stressor, and our reaction to it which lead to the sequence being defined as traumatic stress. The Diagnostic and Statistical Manual (DSM IV), for instance, defines stress as traumatic if (1) the person experienced, witnessed or was confronted with an event or events that involved actual or threatened death or serious injury, or a threat to the physical integrity of self or others, *and* (2) the person's response involved fear, helplessness, or horror.

Our reaction to traumatic stress will depend on a complex interaction between the stressor, the environment, and ourselves as individuals with our own unique histories and personal characteristics. Some events are so horrifying that every imaginable human being would become to some degree disordered as a result of the suffering involved. Other events satisfy the diagnostic criteria, but most people who survive the event do not become disordered afterwards. These are situations in which people are spontaneously able to process the physiological responses and traumatic 'memories' (fragments of sensory experience stored in the limbic system which are precise imprints of a fragment of the horrifying event) and resolve the trauma, which then becomes stored in ordinary narrative memory as an unpleasant event which happened to them in the past.

What is post traumatic stress disorder?
The changes in the brain produced by traumatic stress are permanent. So are the changes in the brain produced by a host of other events, injuries and brain-harming human activities. Most of the time the wonderfully adaptable human brain accommodates more or less seamlessly to the altered pathways, processes and responses available to it, and we carry on our heedless lives blissfully unaware of the scars we wear within.

We humans accommodate to most of the traumas which afflict us. The danger passes, safety is re-established, the wounds heal, traumatic memories are processed, order and reason and meaning are rediscovered, we adapt and recover. Sometimes this does not or cannot happen, the conditions for recovery are never established, or the process of recovery is interrupted, and out of traumatic stress develops the vicious self-perpetuating cycle of post traumatic stress disorder.

Trauma is a complex psychosocial phenomenon. It is possible, of course, to imagine the completely socially isolated individual, the person-on-a-desert-island, suffering traumatic experiences. But without a social context in which to run its course, this would not be trauma as we know it. If our castaway became behaviourally disturbed and started slashing at invisible enemies with a machete, or woke raving and weeping uncontrollably at 3.00 am, there would be no-one there to witness the delirium, no social network to assist or hinder the complex process of adaptation and recovery, no laws to break or social expectations to offend, no loving arms to hold and comfort through the nightmares. The genuinely isolated individual would reach a point of being able to function effectively again, complete or partial recovery, or they would die of suicide or self-neglect. Making no ripple on the sea of humanity, this would not be trauma as it is coming to be understood in medical, psychological, legal and educational practice. For traumatic stress is not a private but a social process. Trauma victims make claims upon us; they must attempt to manage their distress in the midst of our society, and their suffering amongst us cries out for a response.

Recovery from traumatic stress is a complex and complicated psychosocial process. 'It is not just what happens to people that is important, but also what it means to those people in relation to their sense of who they are, the world they live in and what their expectations are for the future' (Joseph et al, 1997). Remembering, of course, that our sense of who we are, our understanding of the world around us, and our expectations, hopes and fears for the future are only partly individual internal cognitive and emotional constructs; they are also external social constructs held within and shaped by the groups and groupings, communities and societies which contain us.

To recover from traumatic stress, the sufferer needs to be in a safe environment, to be part of a secure and accepting social network, and to have the inner and outer resources to manage the physiological and biological reactions of stress and to process and come to terms with the horrifying experience.

If enough of these factors are absent the victim will be unable to recover. If other factors, such as further trauma, intervene the recovering victim may be unable to complete the process of recovery. If the statistics are against them in terms of the nature of the trauma (victims of rape or torture, for instance, are more likely to suffer disorder than victims of floods or volcanic eruptions) then sufferers may be unable to recover.

Those who do not recover from traumatic stress are likely to develop post traumatic stress disorder. This is a deteriorating condition in which the physiological, psychological and social functioning of the victim are seriously impaired. For me the most persuasive description of the onset of post traumatic stress disorder is that which sees the developing disorder as a failure of the normal processes of adaptation to trauma. Horowitz (1976) proposed a model of cognitive processing of traumatic events which has proved helpful in developing an understanding of the onset of the condition. Extended and refined by many over the years, we can now reasonably consider that the normal pattern of cognitive and emotional processing which follows a traumatic event is the same pattern, which, persisting without being resolved, leads on to the vicious circularity of PTSD.

Trauma is wordless terror. Traumatic stress is a flooding of the system with stress hormones at a level which overwhelms our normal thought processes and puts us in an optimum state of preparedness to survive an acute and horrifying emergency. In that state we are disabled from normal functioning since we cannot think, or reason, or enjoy and digest our food, or fall in love, or sleep, or daydream, or play or do anything other than survive or die.

Once the immediate threat recedes, assuming that it does, the levels of stress hormones begin to fall. At that point we have no normal memory of the traumatic event; instead we have a jumble of disconnected sensory impressions and fleeting somatic, emotional and cognitive experiences which are stored just as they happened in our limbic system (Carter, 1998, p95). Since the experience was, by definition, overwhelming, the process of assimilation and recovery is gradual. It is a process of alternating intrusion and avoidance. Intrusion into consciousness of elements of the experience, enabling assimilation into normal cognitive awareness and narrative memory, alternating with avoidance of traumatic memories allowing us to rest and relax between episodes of assimilation and thus preventing overload.

When we recover from traumatic stress this process of intrusion and avoidance goes forward through various phases or cycles (e.g. Joseph *et al*, 1997, p85). When we fail to recover, but instead develop post traumatic stress disorder, the intrusive thoughts, images and sensory impressions become themselves the triggers for a traumatic stress reaction. That is, we respond to the traumatic memory as if it were the original trauma. Since in these circumstances the sensory impressions and images which constitute traumatic memory have become trauma events, the victim is not able to process the original horrifying event and consign it to narrative memory, but instead is actively re-traumatised by the intrusive sensory experience. As this process continues there is a 'kindling' of the limbic system, which becomes progressively more sensitised to experience internal stimuli (traumatic memories) and neutral external stimuli as traumatic threats.

The sufferer becomes locked into a deteriorating cycle of interpreting neutral stimuli as terrifying threats, with a pattern of increasingly phobic responses to objectively harmless events. Ultimately, in severe PTSD, the victim will be phobic to their own thoughts and memories, at which point it is impossible to establish normal life functioning, and a range of emotional and behavioural problems will be inevitable. These problems are often the presenting symptoms which the sufferer brings for help.

The emotional, psychological and behavioural problems which bring victims of PTSD to the attention of clinicians and other practitioners of the healing arts are often far removed from the original trauma, which may itself be excised from memory by traumatic amnesia. What the symptoms have in common, and what will tie them in to a diagnosis of PTSD, is the pattern of intrusion and avoidance which underlies the whole varied range of thoughts, feelings and behaviours, which began after the traumatic event, which persists over time, and which results in significant distress or impairment of personal and social functioning. These are the criteria which must be met before a diagnosis of post traumatic stress disorder will be reached. If indeed a diagnosis of post traumatic stress disorder is ever reached. We know of many, and may guess at many more, sufferers who have spent years living with misdiagnosis and useless treatment, or lifetimes living with labels justifying no treatment at all.

To sum up, if we suffer trauma the traumatic event triggers a response in the limbic system of our brain which is beyond our conscious control. This response very rapidly, almost instantaneously, generates traumatic stress, an intense stress reaction which has the effect of closing down our normal body-mind functioning and priming our system to survive the emergency by overcoming the threat or by making good our escape, the well-known fight or flight response.

The process of recovery from traumatic stress seems to be a cycle of alternately revisiting the trauma and assimilating it, an automatic splitting up of the unbearable experience into manageable fragments which allows the reality of having been the victim of incomprehensible and devastating horror to be integrated into our memory and be rendered harmless.

Factors influencing the course of recovery include: the nature and extent of the trauma; the safety, stability and familiarity of the post trauma environment; secure attachment relationships and a supportive social network; our reactions at the time of the trauma; the adaptability or durability of our personal systems of belief and ways of understanding the world; the nature of our personality before the trauma; our personal or familial history of mental health or illness; the impact of previous, and subsequent, trauma. If these factors, or enough of them, operate in our favour we recover from the traumatic stress. The wound heals, the traumatic experience is integrated harmlessly into our narrative memory, and we discover that we have been changed but not destroyed.

Sometimes people experience acute distress after a traumatic event, with many symptoms of disorder, but the disorder is transitory and self-healing. If this causes sufficient distress to require medical attention, the diagnosis may be one of Acute Stress Disorder, a transient condition of distress and severe functional impairment after trauma with onset within four weeks of the traumatic event and lasting not less than two days and not more than four weeks.

This is different from post traumatic stress disorder, which has a longer latency period, with onset usually a few weeks to a few months after the event (occasionally much later), and a longer duration, lasting not less than one month. Acute post traumatic stress disorder resolves itself within three months, chronic disorder lasts longer than three months and may persist for many years, producing permanent and significant changes in the personality of the sufferer.

Symptoms of post traumatic stress disorder include:

- intrusive re-experiencing
- autonomic hyperarousal
- avoidance of trigger stimuli
- numbing of responsiveness
- intense emotional reactions
- learning difficulties
- memory disturbance
- dissociation
- aggression against self and others
- psychosomatic disorders

Of these, the first three are definitive, and the others are illustrative of a range of symptoms which may be experienced over the course of the disorder (McFarlane and van der Kolk in van der Kolk *et al*, pp420-423)

The criteria for a diagnosis of post traumatic stress disorder are:

- the person must have lived through a traumatic event
- the event, or elements of it, must be re-experienced by the victim as though occurring in the present – intrusive re-experiencing

- the victim must find themselves persistently avoiding stimuli associated with the trauma – avoidance of triggers
- the victim must experience symptoms of increased arousal of the autonomic nervous system, such as panic attacks, exaggerated startle response or hypervigilance, not present before the trauma
- all these symptoms must last for not less than one month
- the symptoms must cause significant distress to the victim or impairment in social, occupational or other important areas of functioning

It is important to remember that our understanding of post traumatic stress disorder is developing and changing all the time. A condition whose existence has been denied or minimised by mainstream psychiatry for a hundred years is difficult to integrate into the belief structures which inform psychiatric diagnosis and treatment. This is particularly noticeable when we venture into the territory of the disorders of childhood and adolescence.

Is childhood trauma different from adult trauma?

The descriptions of trauma, traumatic stress and post traumatic stress disorder so far recounted relate primarily to research on adult populations. As long ago as 1988 Finkelhor was proposing that the after-effects of child sexual abuse should not be regarded as a type of post traumatic stress disorder. He had three main reasons for this.

The first was that he had a perfectly good model of his own to put forward which he regarded as having greater explanatory elegance and predictive validity than a PTSD model for child sexual abuse. There is never anything wrong with turning something down because you believe you have something better to propose.

The second is that only a proportion of people sexually abused as children develop PTSD, therefore the model lacks validity for this population. This is less convincing; trauma is, by definition, an injury, and people react differently to injury, whilst clinically there are broad areas of similarity. Post traumatic stress disorder is the condition which develops in a proportion of a population who have been subject to traumatic stress. I once had a neck injury from which statistically 60% of the injured population recover within five years, and 40% have life-long undiminished symptoms; the progress of my recovery was one of the few times I have been glad to be part of a majority. But that is the nature of human injury; more or less disabled, more or less joyfully surviving, we drift in and out of the statistical tables by which clinicians define their medical priorities.

Finkelhor's third argument for excluding child sexual abuse from post traumatic stress disorder was that the then current descriptions of PTSD failed to encompass or adequately describe the symptoms experienced by survivors of sex abuse. He rightly points out that the definition of PTSD would have to be broadened to accommodate sexual abuse. 'But as the notion of PTSD is broadened, it loses meaning, becoming little more than a list of all the symptoms of mental health impairment, which are, almost by definition, signs of stress. At that point the PTSD concept loses much of its usefulness ...' (Finkelhor in Wyatt and Powell, 1988, p68).

This misses a vital point. The current understanding of trauma represents a quantum leap in the treatment of psychiatric disorder. The concept is indeed broad, and it will grow broader yet, for it is categorically different from what has gone before.

Thirty years ago I was studying physics, or rather, in those days long ago and far away, I was being taught physics. I had been taught about atoms, and molecules, and sub-atomic particles and had absorbed the information well enough to pass the tests. Then one day, almost in parenthesis, the teacher mentioned the Uncertainty Principle of Werner Heisenberg. I can remember now the sense of amazement, a visual experience of a door opening in a monochrome landscape and a momentary glimpse of a world of swirling colour beyond, my first intimations of the delights of chaos. 'Doesn't this change everything?' I asked, but no-one there and then agreed with me.

The psychiatric study of the effects of trauma really does change everything. Mental health impairment has been seen throughout the history of mainstream psychiatry as an inner process in a world in which individuals are clearly defined as existing within, influenced by, but separate from their environment. Many voices have proposed other models of human development (e.g. Bronfenbrenner, 1979, and Shotter, 1984), but these have never been absorbed into psychiatric practice. Some psychiatrists have worked on the principle that mental health problems are generated from the environment (e.g. Laing, 1965), but their attempts to generalise from case experience have been marginalised. The world-wide thinking about trauma and its effects, patchy and incomplete and diverse as it is, marks a genuine transition. If it develops as it has begun, it will change the way we treat one another, for it represents a radical change in our understanding of the interface and interaction between persons and the material and social and cultural environment in which they find themselves.

Trauma theory indicates that events in the environment generate permanent physiological and neurological changes in us, and that these changes in the structure and function of our brains and nervous systems affect the way we think and feel and behave. Trauma research indicates that these changes in structure and function are indeed persistent and measurable, and do correlate to certain patterns of thought and feeling and behaviour. This is a whole new field of thought in psychiatry, and we cannot yet tell how wide its boundaries may stretch. Certainly it is wide enough to incorporate the distressing after-effects of child sexual abuse and other childhood trauma, for the one primary criterion has been met; the distress arises as a result of a real event or events in the outward and visible world, and is not the product solely of intrapsychic processes arising from the repression of unacceptable impulses. The psychiatric rubicon has been crossed.

Yet the problems raised by Finkelhor are persistent, and practitioners and theorists who espouse the view that the results of childhood trauma are a range of disorders which, occurring as they do after traumatic stress, may be classified as post traumatic stress disorder, are well aware that there are difficulties. Children who have experienced childhood trauma develop differently from their non-traumatised peers, but they also exhibit different symptoms and different patterns of thought, feeling and behaviour from traumatised adults.

Return to the basic and demonstrable premise. Traumatic stress etches indelible and recognisable traces in the brain and nervous system, traces which the victim of trauma experiences as symptoms and the rest of us experience as behaviour. The brain of a child is still forming, adult brains are already formed. It is likely that the differences we can see in the history and development of post traumatic syndromes in children and in adults are rooted in this basic developmental difference. 'Continued progress in the field requires 're-introducing' development into the discussion of childhood PTSD' (Pynoos *et al*, in van der Kolk *et al*, 1996, p352).

Children are subject to the same traumatic events as adults. Natural and technological disasters, wars and conflicts, accidents, assaults, rape, torture, exploitation, and being made to witness the violation of others, all happen to children. Yet childhood trauma is different from adult trauma. Physically the injuries of children differ from those of adults and run a different course of healing and recovery. The young body reacts differently to injury, the same blow produces a different wound. It is reasonable to suppose that the same and more will be true for trauma, for the differences between the immature and mature brain and nervous system are even greater than those between the immature and mature body. Children suffer trauma, they experience traumatic stress, but the processes of recovery or deterioration, the nature and course of the disorders which may follow traumatic stress, are somewhat different in childhood from the patterns of adult post traumatic stress recovery or disorder.

One response to the experience of wordless terror which we call traumatic stress is dissociation, a process in which the overwhelmed victim survives the horror by splitting into parts. This ensures that at least part of the victim can be available to react with fight or flight should those become possible, even though the part of the victim experiencing the horrifying event is frozen by shock into immobilization. Dissociation is a fairly common minority response to all traumatic stress, but it seems to be a particularly common response in children, who lack the greater range of self-protective internal defence strategies which may be available to autonomous adults. It seems to be even more common as a response to the trauma caused by paedophilia and network child abuse, where the extreme assaults on bodily integrity and personal space and security, combined with the success of extreme tactics of confusion, mystification, seduction and fear on the part of the perpetrator, are particularly likely to leave the child with no option for trying to contain the experience other than splitting it up into bits by fragmenting the self.

This dissociation can be anything from a splitting off of isolated elements of the event such as the physical pain or the feelings of rage or powerlessness, to the establishment of entirely separate ego states, another self or other selves to whom bad things happen. In children, '... containing aspects of the traumatic experience in a separate ego state can be understood as an exaggeration and fixation of normal developmental processes' (van der Kolk in van der Kolk *et al*, 1996, p193).

The growing child discovers and forms an identity by experimenting and playing with many different identities: good child, bad child, mother, father, teacher, all sorts of possible identities are tried on for size. This process is a normal part of maturing, and only partly within the control of the child, who needs to be able to become fully absorbed in the experimental roles in order to establish a well-founded and deep-rooted sense of identity in adulthood. The child is entirely dependent on surrounding adults to provide safety while this necessary exploration takes place. If that safety collapses, the developing child is left vulnerable indeed. The alternative identities so readily formed at this stage become perfect repositories for the unbearable traumatic experience.

Dissociation at the point of trauma becomes a fixed tendency; once a person has learned to dissociate, that will be their automatic reaction to traumatic stress. It is a successful strategy for immediate survival. Dissociation is also a predictor for the development of post traumatic stress disorder; people who dissociate at the time of trauma are more likely to develop post traumatic stress disorder than those in whom other defence mechanisms are activated.

There are some people who dissociate as a response to traumatic stress for whom the dissociated fragments of experience become dissociated fragments of identity, ego states which are fixed but normally hidden bits of the self containing the dangerous traumatic memories. We have seen that children are generally more likely than adults to respond in this way to trauma. For some people the fragmentation of the self goes further, and the dissociated ego states take on a life of their own, existing side by side in the same personality, the condition known as dissociative identity disorder.

Children subjected to the traumatic stress associated with paedophilia and network child abuse are particularly vulnerable to dissociative disorders which may manifest themselves as, or exist alongside, conditions carrying such diagnoses as borderline personality disorder, somatisation disorder, and major depression. The still forming personality of the growing child cannot contain the fragmenting self.

Do paedophiles cause traumatic stress in children?

Paedophiles arc people who think about having sex with children, people who entertain ideas which are literally unthinkable to many others in the community in which they live and on which they depend. Whether 'fixated' or 'regressive', male or female, rich or poor, outwardly successful and powerful or obviously inadequate and needy, they are people who can experience and sustain sexual arousal of which a child is the object. Most people most of the time do not even want to think about the invisible boundary which paedophiles have crossed. This makes it easier for paedophilia to flourish.

Some people may be paedophiles in this sense of sustaining sexual thoughts and feelings towards children, but never enter into any paedophile activity because they are restrained by their own internal inhibitors and would find the guilt insupportable. There is no way of knowing with certainty that such people exist. Self reporting will be unreliable, since again the powerful internal and external inhibitors around paedophilia generate massive cognitive distortions which make it extremely difficult to determine facts let alone truth in this area. Not to mention the fact that sometimes people tell lies, and people who are abusing children tell lies a lot.

Social exclusion makes for group cohesion. Given the strength and power of the inhibitors around paedophilia, it is inevitable that paedophiles will become organised and create an internally cohesive and validating social group. The extent of organised paedophile activity in our community is beginning to emerge, despite all the forces operating to keep it secret.

The intention here is to consider the impact of paedophilia and network child abuse. In this sense paedophilia is to be regarded as the organised activities of people whose sexual orientation is wholly or partly towards children. Not all organised paedophiles work in rings or networks, lone paedophiles may be highly organised and purposeful in their activity (Gaspar and Bibby in Bibby, 1996, p50). Network child abuse is distinguished as a separate category for this reason and also because not all people involved in abusive networks are paedophiles, the buying and selling of young bodies being a highly commercial operation.

This is a journey of discovery, an exploration of the traumatic effects of paedophile activity on various groups of people. Thus it is necessary to determine whether there is evidence that children who are the objects of paedophile activity suffer traumatic stress as a result. If they do not, then there is no territory to explore.

There are no reliable figures on the extent of paedophile activity in our society. There are figures available on sexual offences against children, but it is difficult to define from these what constitutes organised abuse, and impossible to do anything more than guess at the prevalence of activities which are never detected as offences. Statistics in this field are meaningless, and will remain so until as a society we have a better grasp of the issues involved.

Consider the following references: 'Given the estimate by the US Department of Justice that every year 250,000 children are sexually abused ...' (McFarlane and van der Kolk in van der Kolk *et al*, 1996, p38). 'Studies of the general population of adults show that anywhere from 6% to 63% of females were sexually abused as children' (child abuse and neglect statistics from the National Committee to Prevent Child Abuse, USA, 1995). And in Britain 'The National Commission of Inquiry into the Prevention of Child Abuse reviewed the current state of our knowledge. It estimated that ... up to 100,000 [children] each year have a potentially harmful sexual experience' (Utting, 1997, p16). 'A survey of police forces, Social Services Departments, and the NSPCC in England and Wales covering the four-year period from January 1988 to December 1991 produced an estimated national incidence rate for organised abuse of 967 cases over four years, or an average of 242 cases per year, but no data on pornography (Catherine Itzin in Bibby 1996, p173); and, in chapter sixteen, 'Having said this, it was believed that many agencies had reported to the survey only a small proportion of cases that were known to them' (Gallagher, Hughes and Parker in Bibby 1996, p218). We really do not know how many people are victims of paedophile abuse as children.

All we can be sure of is that paedophilia involves children being sexually abused, and we do know quite a lot about the effects of child sexual abuse, although again we can have no way of knowing how complete our picture is. Our understanding of the effects of sexual abuse is built on work with adult survivors and work with children who are known to have been victims. From that limited population we can build a picture of the effects of such abuse. Finkelhor, who in 1988 was so vehement in wishing to exclude the disorders which follow child sexual abuse from being described as post traumatic stress disorder, was equally vehement in arguing that sexual abuse generates trauma.

His 'Traumagenic Dynamics Model' (Finkelhor in Wyatt and Powell, 1988, p68) proposes four dynamics to explain the impact of sexual abuse on the developing child. Taken together the dynamics of traumatic sexualization, betrayal, stigmatization and powerlessness distort the child's understanding of themselves and of the world around them and damage the capacity of the child to relate to self and others. These distortions generate traumatic stress which in turn leads to disorders of thought, feeling and behaviour.

This theory has proved a useful working tool for many entrusted with the care or therapy of children who have suffered sexual abuse. Trauma theory based on research into post traumatic stress disorder would suggest that the trauma precedes the cognitive and emotional distortion, but either way the result is that the sexual abuse of children produces traumatic stress for the child.

The first critical factor in determining that an emotional or behavioural disorder may be considered as a post traumatic disorder is that it arises from injury and not from illness. Since it is accepted that paedophile abuse causes traumatic stress in children, that the abuse is a traumatic event which injures the child, it is reasonable to expect that some people who are victims of such abuse will develop post traumatic stress disorder.

I suspect that the casualty rate in such abuse is high, but it will be a long time before research can realistically confirm or disprove my suspicion. In these early days of the uncovering of paedophile abuse, the statistics do not matter much; there is an injury which disables some people who suffer it. That is the significant thing to recognise. It then becomes possible and necessary to examine both the injury and the disabilities it produces.

Chapter 3

Fragments

'Then there was the pain. A breaking and entering when even the senses are torn apart. The act of rape on an eight-year-old body is a matter of the needle giving because the camel can't. The child gives, because the body can, and the mind of the violator cannot.' *I Know Why the Caged Bird Sings,* Virago Press, 1984, Maya Angelou (p.76)

'All children .... need a wide range of friendships with loving adults outside their own family prepared to treat them increasingly as equals. Our social and sexual conventions .... too often deny children these vital experiences. I do not contend that paedophiles should be recruited in large numbers to supply them; but I have argued that, if a child does develop a warm relationship with a paedophile which includes shared sexual pleasure, the sex is unlikely to do the child much harm, and the friendship may well be more beneficial than otherwise. ... a wise parent may well not insist on bringing the relationship to an end ...' *Perspectives on Paedophilia,* Batsford Academic, 1981, edited by Brian Taylor, Chapter 2, 'The Adult', Peter Righton, Director of Education, NISW (p39)

Dreams and shadows – memories of a woman in middle age
When I was six I dreamed of fire. Leaping, dancing, roaring it devoured the big boys' school, big as a village, our next door neighbour and the centre of my world. As the fire roared, I also leapt and danced. Flames soared, sparks flew like fireworks, like burning arrows, high into the air and landed ... on our house. Now joy turned to terror, as I ran and screamed 'Take care! Take care! The fire will eat our home!' But my parents, innocently sleeping, could not hear.

They would have saved me if they could. If I had been a good child I would have been safe. The big boys told me that. Only bad children do the things the grown ups do, only evil children behave like the animals, only those who are already set apart and marked as different will be chosen to join this special club, this band of friends who soon became my only friends. 'She has so much to learn' my father had said, meaning that

29

animals are educational. But 'We're going to teach you' the big boys said, holding me down in the dung-sweet straw, and I was lost, never knowing if this was the much I had to learn.

They used my long hair, my mother's pride of braids, to hold me while they used me. 'Give us a head-fuck, girl. Give us your mouth.' Words I never heard elsewhere they used. I tried it once at home, 'Fuck' I said, and found it would not do to share what I had learned.

Later they held me down to teach me more of what they had been taught themselves ten years before when they were just my age, lessons repeated down the years, learned to perfection, ready to pass on. 'We're going to teach you to like it. And if you do, then we'll know you're one of us and not a normal child at all.' So by degrees I learned where I belonged, and how to recognise my friends.

I learned so much. I learned to tell no lies explaining injuries, but made a friend of gravity; I fell from trees, I fell from walls, and once, when walking had become a problem, I climbed a five-barred gate, fell straddled, and ran home to cry at last.

The child's story – OUTRAGE

As I recall, I couldn't have wanted for anything, any material thing that is to say. 'Spoiled', people would have said, 'the child is spoiled', but you never can tell what goes on within the family.

I wanted to be loved, to be able to trust, to be a normal little girl. I know I didn't want the sexually perverted relationship that was pushed on me from an early age. Yes, I can remember back as far as three and four, not good memories, only the hurtful ones I carry everywhere, ready to be triggered at any time.

It's hard when you're young to know wrong from right, but somewhere deep inside I knew it all was wrong. At the same time, you're just a kid, you don't really have a voice to speak. And what do you say if you can find the courage? You're scared, you're hurting, and you're alone. It's the worst feeling ever, but knowing it has to stop is one thing, knowing how to stop it is another.

I didn't find my voice until I was thirteen. Those years were the longest and most hurtful. That will always stay with me, no matter where I am, or who I pretend to be.

Not only did he take the innocent childhood I should have had, but he also left me a huge depressing chip on my shoulder which each day reminds me of the pain.

This and the two poems which follow were written by Marie Gilbert.

Silent Screams

I'm looking in his eyes,
But he's a different guy.
As if he's split,
Yes, into two.
His eyes are cold,
I never noticed before,
Maybe because I haven't ever been this close.
His mouth moves,
I'm struggling,
I don't want to hear his words,
Just want to be alone.
I'm crying now
My silent screams
So loud,
I thought
Nobody heard
Or maybe they prefer not to.
His touch
Makes me shudder,
Scared and warned.
I sit here all alone,
Alone at last,
My heart throbbing,
My eyes stinging,
My head spinning,
Hoping that maybe
That was the last time.

It was like he took my
Voice and threatened
My ears after abusing
My body and thought
It was all right.

Something was wrong.
But a scared little girl
Didn't have a voice.
Sadness streaked her eyes.
Presents we're given
Instead of love.
Trapped ... Mute ... Unhappy
Until I took a chance.
I'd had enough.
I found my voice
A pair of ears.
Brave, they say.
Alone, unloved, fearing my own shadow
Now
I will talk
People will listen.
My body is finally mine.

A song on the breeze – memories of a young woman

A song on the breeze –

'Ashamed' and 'abused'

Are my middle names.

I cannot hide

Like you from a shadow.

Scared as a mouse

Trapped in a web

Where time never heals.

An innocent voice

Feels so much guilt.

One little girl

Held so many secrets

And can never hold

Her head up high again.

The carer's story – RAGE

I carried you screaming, face red and twisted with rage, back arched, legs kicking, arms flailing, and laid you on the settee, placed cushions on the floor in case you fell, and waited. Much later, still wracked with the occasional sob, you came and climbed on my knee. 'I wanted an ice cream and you wouldn't let me have one.' 'That's right.' 'And then I wanted to kill you.' 'Yes.' Snuggling closer, 'Are you all right, mum?' 'Yes. I'm fine.' Long pause. 'Can I have an ice cream now?'. 'No. But you can have a drink if you'd like one.' Silence so long I think you might have fallen asleep. 'Can I have a drink, please?'.

'It was my job to look after the babies. But I got really tired and fell asleep. When he came back my dad dragged me out of bed and belted me, buckle end. After that he said I was useless, so he just lent me to his friends when they wanted me.' 'How old were you then?' 'Five, I think. Maybe six.'

A day in foster care

We have a meeting today. Kelly has left us. 'Run away,' her social worker says. 'Run to ..' seems more the shape of it to me. Kelly agrees with me. At the children's home they asked her 'So what went wrong at your foster home, then?' 'Nothing,' says Kelly, 'I just wanted to go home.'

That 'nothing' of course does not take account of the tantrum we had to deal with, although I am still smarting from the bruises indicating the difference between two and thirteen when it comes to managing major outbursts of rage.

The meeting is to be held in the conference room, a grand title for a tatty office with a big table in the middle. Everyone seems to be there when we arrive; social worker, senior social worker, father, step-mother, and the two of us. Everyone? 'Where's Kelly?' I ask. In the outer office looking after the latest batch of babies, her social worker explains. I protest. Rather angrily, the social worker opens the door and shouts out 'Kelly! Do you want to come in here and join the meeting, or stay there and look after your brothers?' 'I'll stay out here.' The social worker looks at me as though she has won a point, though I'm not quite sure what it might be.

We carry on with the meeting. I describe the difficulties Kelly seems to experience around contact with home. How often following telephone calls from home we have incidents of violence or self-harm. How last week just such an incident occurred after Kelly had a telephone call telling her that her brother was in hospital after falling from a swing. How she has described vivid memories of bruises in her own early childhood being frequently explained as the results of accidents; that falling off swings was a particularly common explanation given in these circumstances.

Dad has picked up just one word from my report. 'Violence?' he says 'What violence? My daughter's not violent.' I pull down my roll neck jumper a little to show the now fading bruises on my neck and shoulders. He studies these with the eyes of a connoisseur. 'Well that's not violence,' he pronounces, 'that's just hitting people.'

Kelly has made a statement to her social worker. She has said she feels confused and upset. That she wants to live with us, but that she also wants to look after her brothers and sister. However, since returning to her home area has simply left her living in a children's home, and no-one has any intention of letting her go back to live with her family, she would like to come back and live with us. She also said that she was sorry for getting in such a temper and lashing out at me.

We have a statement from all the family saying that we want to have Kelly back, but that we would like the social services department to take more active responsibility for ensuring that Kelly's brothers and sister stay safe, so that she can leave that burden behind her. The senior social worker assures us that they are fully aware of their responsibilities, and doing everything possible within the resources available to them.

The decision is made that Kelly will return to us. This is happy news. Less hopeful is the fact that absolutely nothing else in the situation looks like changing, except that some assurances have been given.

In the car on the way home Kelly maintains an endless flow of meaningless chatter. Eye contact produces a sweet and dazzling smile. She is evidently as happy as a child can be. I run through a mental checklist. Tablets locked up; knives locked away; chemicals all safely stored; I think we have it all covered.

Arriving in time for the evening meal, Kelly is delighted to see everyone again. She might have been away a year instead of a week, so excited and pleased is she to be home. Throughout the meal she chatters on about friends in school, the latest gossip, television programmes she has seen and those she has missed. The others take the barrage good-naturedly, pleased to have her back, whilst reminding themselves of the need to put earplugs on their next shopping list.

Later the whole group get drawn into their own idiosyncratic version of hide and seek, and the evening passes cheerfully till supper time. Now suddenly Kelly is pale and quiet, sipping milk and nibbling at biscuits which the others are consuming with gusto. I look across at Colin, note that he too has registered the change, is on the alert. 'I'm going to get ready for bed. 'Night,' she says, and disappears.

Within seconds we hear the sound of heavy dragging, followed by a crash. Both of us run for the stairs. Her door is closed, and blocked by some piece of furniture dragged across it. We can hear her sobbing, but she makes no response to me as I call her name. Colin fetches David and Rachel. Sometimes Kelly will respond to Rachel when she has gone beyond hearing the rest of us. 'Come on, Kelly, it's me,

Rachel. Open the door, love.' 'I can't, Rae, I've had it. I can't do any more.' Then suddenly, shouting, 'I hate him, Rae, I fucking hate him. I wish he'd killed me when he had the chance.'

Together we force the door open enough for Rachel and me to squeeze in. You can lock away the drugs and the knives, but light bulbs shatter into sharp and cruel edges. Her hands and arms are bleeding profusely. Rachel pulls the chest of drawers away from the door, David arrives with a clean towel, Colin takes a pillow and a duvet to the car, and we set off for the casualty unit fifteen miles away.

I hold her in my arms all the way there. She shivers and occasionally sobs, but has finally gone beyond words. In the hospital they remove remaining fragments of glass, and dress her wounds. We point out that this is self-inflicted and that we believe that Kelly is still very angry and upset; is there any possibility of a referral for psychiatric assessment, we ask. With the resources available, injuries like this, which do not constitute attempted suicide, do not merit automatic referral. We are offered the option of going to our GP and asking for a referral to the waiting list, currently standing at about nine months. We try to picture what Kelly might be doing in nine months time.

At home, all of us by now very sleepy, we help her up to bed. I lean over and kiss her forehead. 'Good night, sweetheart, remember we all love you.' From somewhere she summons a cheeky grin, 'Just as well really, innit? 'Night.'

In my dreams, I retaliate. Smash. Batter to a pulp. Ferocious violence pours through me. I wake refreshed and relaxed, grateful for the versatility of the human mind.

'I did hate you, mum.' 'Yes.' 'I wanted to kill you.' 'Yes, you did.' 'And now I love you.' 'I know. I love you too. Sleep well.'

Dreams and shadows revisited – memories of a man in middle age

When I was sixteen I knew that I was evil. No memory of the teachers of my younger childhood would ever surface now. Only the space remained where memory should have been, the space I called the Pit, and smelled the sulphur when I stepped too close to the edge of the abyss.

I tried to kill myself. After the third time, they took me to see a psychiatrist. He said 'This young man is insane', which I believed, oh yes. At first they tried to lock me up, but I learned how to give them better answers, and went to live outside again. Then I became two people. On the outside a successful, lying self who won the prize at school and went to university. On the inside a creature lurking in the shadows, waiting to appear at every unguarded moment of the day, and always in the dead hours of the night.

I became a thief. I stole from shops because I could, and never once was caught. It was my hobby, the skill in evading all security as potent a producer of thrills as my school and college contemporaries found in sport or chasing girls.

I became an addict. Where others turned to alcohol or heroin, I became hooked on dangerous sex. I was a pretty boy, and I could pick up men in the least as well as the most likely places. My eye was unerring, my instinct for picking those in whose company I felt at home was absolute, and always I would get involved with partners who would satisfy my lust for danger to the brink of death.

It was, I discovered, the body that knew what the mind could not remember. I had thought I was as together as I would ever be, then, out of nowhere, learning to move differently, the body told the story. A lifetime since those days when he abused me, yet the body's memories were as clear as yesterday. At first I could not believe what my own self was teaching me. I checked, followed clues and leads, until I knew with certainty that every word of the new story I was telling myself, the new story of my life, was true. And how shall I live now?

> Not, I'll not, carrion comfort, Despair, not feast on thee;
> Not untwist − slack they may be − these last strands of man
> In me or, most weary, cry I can no more. I can;
> Can something, hope, wish day come, not choose not to be.
>
> But ah, but O thou terrible, why wouldst thou rude on me
> Thy wring-earth right foot rock? lay a lionlimb against me? Scan
> With darksome devouring eyes my bruisëd bones? And fan,
> O in turns of tempest, me heaped there; me frantic to avoid thee and flee?
>
> 'Carrion Comfort', Gerard Manley Hopkins

A social worker wrote:
You stare from somewhere
Under your eyes.
Your half smile
Is mere politeness.
No-one believed you
Over fifteen years.
They thought you were
Weird
In fearing blood.
But he was such a nice friend
To you.
So perfectly respectable,
So plausible.
He gave you so much.
So many outings and sports activities
To a
Poor deprived child.

No-one saw the volumes
Of naked photographs.
Album upon album.
He had created you
For him.

When the police
Finally got him
You were angry.
The creation was outraged.
Because now you would have to see if
You were anywhere to be
Found.

by *Liz Davies*

Chapter 4

Communicating Chaos
actions speak louder than words

'The only thing I could do was to stop talking .... Just my breath, carrying my words out, might poison people ..... I had to stop talking.' *I Know Why the Caged Bird Sings*, Virago Press, 1984, Maya Angelou (p.85)

We do not communicate much in words. To begin with we have no words at all, as new born babies our world, we may guess, is all about smell and touch, taste and sound. Throughout childhood our grasp of language grows and develops, until by the time we are adult our world is dominated by words. When we are with other people, attempting to communicate with them, quite a chunk of that communication takes place through the medium of words. Even when we try to communicate feelings, perhaps as much as a massive ten per cent of our adult communication takes place through words; the rest is non-verbal (see Goleman, 1996, p97).

Children are only part of the way on that journey to language. Subjected to the wordless terror of trauma it is reasonable to assume that it is much more difficult for a child than for an adult to reach a point of being able to resolve the trauma through the healing power of words.

Sexual abuse is particularly likely to leave children speechless. They are silenced by their own terror, by their own sense of self-blame and self-loathing, by their own lack of an appropriate vocabulary, and by the threats issued by their abusers. In the case of organised abuse, the perpetrators are likely to be particularly skilled at silencing children. Many adult survivors of paedophilia speak and write movingly of the experience of being silenced as a child.

The silenced child is not telling us of the traumatic stress they have suffered. Instead those who care for them live with the disorders which indicate the unspoken terrors, the painful distortions of thought and feeling and behaviour which afflict the victim of trauma.

The carer's story – FEAR

'Time for bed.' 'But the fox might eat me.' 'Which fox?' 'The one in my room.' We search the room together, trusting small hand gripping mine. Under the bed, in the cupboard, behind the curtains. 'I think he's not here. You can go to bed now.' Three-year-old's bedtime rituals complete, I give a goodnight kiss. 'Sleep well. Sweet dreams.' "Night, mum. Leave the light on.'

'When I was five, my dad used to belt me every day. And I was, like, really violent at school. So they sent me away to a boarding school. I was six then. At that place, if I shouted out in the night, I was dragged out of bed and put in a little room called the snug. Just a stone floor and nothing to do. Once there was snow outside, and I was left there from half past five in the morning until breakfast time.'

The following account first appeared in *The Guardian* (1 May 1996).

Another day in foster care

Begin, as I must, with the scream in the dark. One terrified cry 'no .. o .. o!' Threads of fear from the nightmare reach out through the house, chilling me in my warm bed. I grope for the clock; just after three, not the worst night we've had. Wait now, five minutes, ten minutes; then the coughing starts. Five minutes more and a tap at the door.

I go out to the landing. He is fourteen years old, taller than me by a full head, all bones and adolescent angles, shy placatory smile warding off peril. 'Sorry to wake you. I can't sleep. This cough is terrible. Can you give me something for it?' The smile is belied by the eyes – dear God, who left you with terrors like this? – it hurts me to look at his eyes. I put an arm around him, 'It's all right, I don't sleep much, you go back to bed and I'll bring you a warm drink.'

When I arrive with the drink, he is huddled under the covers in a foetal position, shivering. The room smells of fresh cigarette smoke, the window wide open and letting in a gale.

Closing the window, 'I thought perhaps you'd had a bad dream?' 'No. I never dream. It's just this cough that woke me.' 'Do you think you'll sleep now?' 'Mm.' 'Well, I'll be awake for a while. Come and find me if you need me.'

Back in my warm, safe bed, Colin snuggles up to me. 'One of Jay's nightmares?' 'Yes.' 'Will you wait till he's settled?' 'Yes, I'll read for a while.' As dawn breaks, I know we've had an easier night than some, and drift off to sleep.

By seven the others are tucking into breakfast, relishing the one time of day they know they can share untroubled. 'Bad night?' – this from Rachel, over her shoulder, bleached blonde hair skimming her cereal as she does a quick check, registers baggy eyes and dragging feet. 'Aren't they all?'

'Let him sleep,' she says, 'give us some peace. I'll drop him at school on my way to work.' 'Can I have a lift too?' this from Tim, a few months younger than Jay, vulnerable I know, but what can I do? 'If you don't want your bike at school.' I watch him thinking, weighing the issues, even a simple lift become complicated.

'No, I'll ride.' And he reaches over, punches David on the arm 'Check my maths for me?' Gentle David looks up from his otherworld, slaps his little brother – tall as he is and twice as wide – on the back of the head. 'Bring it to my room. We'll have a look at it.' They amble amiably away. Rachel hugs me. 'You take Jay a drink, and I'll get one for Dad.'

I knock on the door and go in. In sleep I can see his face clearly, his features relaxed, his expression peaceful. Waking, tension distorts and bunches the lines of his face, his eyes never free from terror or rage. I lean over and touch him gently on the shoulder, waking him softly, 'Jay, a drink for you.' Anything sharper and he will spring into life as a soldier under fire will wake to a sound. He opens his eyes and smiles, 'Mum! Thanks.' I'm not, but in the half sleep it's close enough, and all the comfort he'll have.

Now there's no rest till he's ready for school. He is as needy as a baby, as dependent as an infant, as touchy as a toddler. 'Where's my ...?' 'Who's got ...?' 'Somebody's taken my ...!' The others go to earth, waiting for the morning storm to pass. At last Rachel shoos him out the door, and David and Tim emerge, still arguing differential equations, to make their own less frazzled way to school.

A quick coffee with Colin, and I'm at the telephone for my morning call, so routine by now I could put it on a tape recorder, responses and all. We need help with this child. Promises were made to us, all of them broken, that we should have full support, everything we needed to make the placement work.

There was a time in our work when such promises meant something, when we safely took into our home and our hearts children whose battered lives and wounded spirits could find comfort and healing in a peaceful environment. But those days have gone, now the same needs stretch us to the limit and beyond, as those who once supported us have had their own work redefined. Once we could share the burden, which then became no burden; now priorities have changed, services reduced, and we are left dangerously exposed as the objects of attachment for seriously wounded children.

'She's in a meeting at the moment. I'll ask her to ring you.' 'Tell her it's urgent.' (Tell her I'm falling apart. Tell her we're desperate. TELL HER TO READ MY LETTERS!) 'She'll ring you within an hour.' I say thank you nicely, the way I was taught, but know I won't be holding my breath for the 'phone call. Promises butter no parsnips, speaking of which, there are things to be doing.

A few tasks on, and the telephone rings. A miracle? No, the school head of year. Jay has attacked a boy during the games lesson, and needs to be picked up. Ever since his last suicide attempt, when the psychiatrist said he was too traumatised for psychotherapy to be anything but dangerous, Jay has been accepted at school on the basis of a special arrangement whereby if things get too tough he can come home at any time.

At school, Jay is with the nurse. This attack, unlike others, was actually minor. Friends saw Jay start to 'flip' and held him back from doing any great damage. But he is sitting huddled in the chair, shaking uncontrollably and hot to the touch. 'I'm sorry! I'm sorry! I didn't mean to!' Then he looks up, searches my face, 'I wanted to kill him. I really wanted to kill him. What's wrong with me?' I can't answer that, certainly not now, not here. The school staff have been wonderful; he is so able, so eager to learn and do well, they have made space for him, and, so far, he has not been excluded. Let's not push our luck. I soothe him, thank them, and take him home.

Five minutes in the car, and the verbal torrent starts. My driving, my looks, my age, my relationship with Colin, my tastes, my friends, all are targets for the stream of jibes. I stonewall, focus my attention on the person behind the words, stay peaceable. As we get into the house, I stop him, turn him to face me, 'You're pushing me, Jay. Why are you doing that?' 'It's fun. Winding the staff up – it's what I'm good at.' 'So what happens then?' 'They send you away. Send you to your room. Tell you to get out of the Unit.' 'Do you want me to send you away?' 'NO!'

I look at him and smile. He grins, laughs, grabs me in a bear hug. 'You're too little to hug properly.' 'Perhaps you're too big. You should have been with us sooner. Lots of child-hugs on offer here.' He moves away from me, looks me full in the face, 'I got lost on the way.' Ain't *that* the truth.

Peaceful now, we make cakes for tea. Yet still he is anxious, scanning my face and body language constantly for signs of displeasure, checking his progress with the simple tasks, belittling his own abilities. Then the mood changes, tension begins to build. I glance at the clock; the others will soon be home, more people to relate to, more mistakes to make.

I leave him clearing up and go to water the hanging baskets, knowing he will follow. As he comes round the side of the house, I spray him with water. Our game. He runs, and I chase him. He laughs, shouts, grabs me and wrestles the spray from me. Now he chases, I run. He catches me and sprays me. 'Right,' I say, 'we're quits now.' His face sets, he whisks the top from the spray and empties a stream of water over my head, drenching me. Then he steps back, trembling, begging me with his eyes not to be angry. 'Did I win?' 'Yes, Jay, you won.' 'Is that all right? You're not angry?' 'It's fine, Jay. It's a game. Now why don't you go and see if you can win against the computer?' He runs off happily, and I go and change my clothes.

Back in the kitchen, Tim arrives home and I ask, 'Good day?' 'So so. Where's Jay?' Always the first question. 'Playing on the computer.' He can relax now, slumped down, long legs stretched out, munching fresh cakes and chatting about school, the casting for the school play, what to take as an audition piece. David arrives, both boys love to be on stage, wander off together to rehearse.

Rachel and Colin arrive together as the meal is ready. Both look the question they will not ask in case the news is bad. I tell them about the attack in school, no injuries this time, Jay calmed down by an after-noon at home. Rachel goes to fetch the boys, David lost in a book, Tim and Jay now playing together on the computer.

For once the meal goes calmly, no tantrums, no upsets. We enjoy each other's company. During washing up, though, Jay begins to niggle at Tim, punching, pinching, flicking with the tea towel. Tim takes it for a while, then goes off to watch television. I listen, but it sounds as though things have settled; leaving the household to its own devices, I curl up in an armchair with coffee and a crossword puzzle.

Colin, angrily, 'That boy is nothing but a walking bloody penis!' We stare at one another, appalled. The way we learn what we already knew. 'I just meant he's so arrogant, so cocky, you know?' I do know, exactly. What, specifically, provoked this, though? Half an hour of non-stop baiting of Tim, who at last has gone to his room, too angry to talk to anyone. 'Do something, Liz, talk to Jay. Get him to back off.' Colin shakes his head, bewildered, used to taking an equal part but here frustrated and held at a distance by Jay's evident and intractable fear of all men.

I sigh, and go to look for Jay. Finding him in the living room, staring into space, I say I need to talk to him. He glares at me. I start in on how he's been pushing at Tim again, making his life unbearable, about how we need to respect one another, and give one another breathing space. Suddenly he shouts 'I don't understand! What do you want? I don't know what you want from me! Do you want a fucking blow job or what?'

I'm speechless. Then he looks at me, sees me at last. 'You've gone red. What is it? What's the matter?' 'I'm embarrassed and angry,' I say, as calmly as I can. 'I'm embarrassed because you've crossed that line we've talked about before. You can talk to me about anything, including sex, but you may not talk to me as though I was your age, or anything other than I am. I am an adult who is responsible for you and who cares for you, and I take that responsibility seriously. I will not abuse you and nor will anyone here. Do you understand me?' Face hidden in a cushion, voice thick with tears. 'Yes.'

'I'm angry because I've been trying to talk to you about not hurting other people, and you are not listening to me. You have been pushing Tim beyond the limit, and you have to stop. Are you listening to me now?' 'Yes. I know it's wrong. I'm sorry.' Then suddenly, bursting out, 'It's just, Tim's like me, you know, I feel close to him, I feel I have the right.' 'So you feel close to Tim, he reminds you of yourself, so you feel it is all right to treat him as you've been treated?' 'A bit. Yes.'

Now the cushion comes down from the face. He acknowledges that he does not have the right to make Tim a victim, and does not truly want to do so. We discuss strategies for his coping. Using the punchbag. Going for a bike ride. Going to his room. I know he means it, know too that the problem for him is in recognising his own actions, coming to terms with his own moods and the feelings which drive him.

'Can I go to Youth Club?' 'Of course.' 'I don't think I ... My foot hurts, can I have a lift?' I smile at him. 'It wasn't too painful for football earlier. What's the real problem?' 'You know.' 'Say it, Jay. It's nothing to be ashamed of.' 'I get scared. You know. Walking on my own.' 'Then I'll give you a lift. Go and get ready.'

At half past nine I pick him up from the Club. Park at the other side of the car park to see him walk across. Pretty steady on his feet. Test the air as he gets into the car, marijuana, I think, no sign of anything stronger tonight. A few days ago it was petrol ('Hey, I've discovered the meaning of life. It's something to do with ..', puzzled, ' .. roundabouts?') Before that it was speed, acid, sometimes ecstasy, sometimes alcohol. Colin says 'Where does he get the money?' Another remark that leaves us staring at each other, speechless.

At home, he gets ready for bed, comes down in his dressing gown, limping. 'My foot really does hurt.' 'What's wrong with it?' 'I think it's .. what do you call it .. an ingrowing toenail. Will you look at it for me?' I go with him to the bathroom. The toe has been hacked and chopped about, is oozing blood and pus. 'What happened here?' 'I was trying to stop it from hurting.' I wash it gently and put on a dressing, then send him off to bed. 'Come up and say goodnight?' 'Of course, if you like.'

Downstairs, Colin has opened a bottle of wine for us to share with Rachel. David and Tim wander down to watch the News with us and share a quiet half hour. This night unusually peaceful. No police on the doorstep. No sitting up waiting for the worst effects of substance abuse to pass. No storms and tantrums, leaving windows and doors to repair. Just a little time to relax and draw breath before we see what nightmares the new night may bring.

But first, a promise to keep. I tap on the door. He is sitting in bed, sticking football stickers in a scrapbook. His music is on, but not too loud. It really is an unusually peaceful night. I kiss him on the forehead. 'Good night, sweetheart. Remember we all love you.'

'I know. Thanks. I love you too. Leave the light on.'

Chapter 5

Secondary Victimisation
Living with the chaos

Foster carers and their families live with children who are living with the experience of post traumatic terror all day and every day for long periods. They have not been part of the abusive system in which the child was previously held, and yet they discover that the system has moved into their home with the child. This experience can be devastating for foster families; it can be even more bewildering and lead to even greater stresses for children and their families when the child is not in foster care. If the abuse took place outside the family, and the family did not knowingly collude in the abuse and is subsequently able to provide a safe environment for the child, then the child's family will become the arena in which the child victim will recover or will live out the continuing revictimisation of post traumatic stress disorder.

The observations of those who thus live closely alongside the silenced child, family, carers, therapist, teachers, and social workers, are vital if we are to recognise how the child who cannot speak the pain is nonetheless expressing it. Over the years I have listened to the stories of many people entrusted with the care and treatment of children who have been victims of paedophile abuse. I have worked with children and their families, with foster families, and with staff in residential homes for children. As a carer myself, I have lived with children who have been the victims of such trauma, keeping them company as they make their own journeys of exploration, discovery and survival. I have compared my own perceptions with those of many others, and have found that there is so much in common that it is worthwhile discerning themes and patterns.

How, then, have the symptoms of post traumatic stress disorder manifested themselves in children I have known and loved? In the behaviour of the child, in the responses I can observe the child eliciting from other people, and in the feelings generated in me by living alongside the child and learning to love them. Let us consider in turn each of the recognised symptoms of PTSD (van der Kolk, McFarlane and van der Hart in van der Kolk *et al*, 1996, pp421-423) and set them alongside my own experience of traumatised children.

Intrusive re-experiencing
Nightmares and night terrors are both frequent and common, and may be traced to traumatic events out of waking memory. Children who are victims of paedophilia may be in such a state of terror that night time itself becomes terrifying. Then the clock watching of exhausted adults longing for bedtime becomes nothing but empty optimism, as energy levels which should be reducing in preparation for the child to sleep instead build up unbearably in preparation for the unidentified and unspeakable horror of the night.

Many ordinary events may act as triggers generating 'flashbacks', episodes of engulfing sensory overload unrelated to the objective perception of the current environment or event. I have seen such episodes triggered by visual stimuli (a green car, a black beard, a camera), sounds (a baby crying, heavy breathing after exertion), smells (disinfectant, blood), touch stimuli (a touch on the shoulder, washing hair), and the taste or texture of food (soft boiled eggs, milk puddings).

Situations in which it seems to be the whole situation, rather than a particular sensory aspect of it, which triggers the overwhelming fragment of memory are too numerous to give more than an idea of the range. Bedtime, using the toilet, menstruation, having an erection, going for a walk with an adult, preparing to go on holiday, sharing a meal, hearing adults arguing, activities associated with religion, the death of an animal, being given a treat or present, birthdays, Christmas, games lessons, and so on and so on.

The common characteristic is not found in the external event but in the reaction of the child. This is one of either terror or rage or some combination of the two. People around the child can sense the unbearable building of tension, which causes discomfort for the observers as well as the child. Sometimes this discomfort in the observer may occur before, or even instead of, any apparent reaction in the child. The discomfort experienced by those in close proximity to the sufferer can lead to social isolation and rejection, even when the child has learned to control and manage their own behavioural responses and is producing no obvious antisocial behaviour.

Remember that the victim of post traumatic stress disorder has lost the language of feelings. As, at the moment of trauma, the pathways in the brain which allow us to put words to our feeling experiences close down, so for the sufferer from post traumatic stress disorder the loss of the ability to express feelings in words, and indeed the loss of ability to experience feelings as anything other than overwhelming somatic states, is enduring.

We may guess that children who suffer trauma do not have a well-developed language of feelings beforehand. Recovery is so much the more difficult as helpers struggle to enable the child to develop a language for emotional experiences which are themselves outside the knowledge of the child. Feelings such as trust, grief, anger, fear, and joy are vital components of human life without which our lives are stunted, our spirits are diminished, and we can neither establish nor maintain loving relationships. These feelings will not develop and allow recovery to begin until the child can locate the feeling and anchor it to language.

The process reminds me of Annie Sullivan's work with the deaf and blind Helen Keller. And Helen Keller's later descriptions of the world of deafness and blindness at a time in history when there was no adequate understanding of the needs arising from such sensory impairment, remind me of the world as it must seem to children who have suffered devastating serial trauma.

In adult life there are a whole range of new triggers waiting to cause intrusive re-experiencing for the sufferer from childhood post traumatic stress disorder as a result of paedophilia. Sexual relationships, having a baby, sexual arousal in self and others, pornographic images, the smell and taste of alcohol, the experience of using mind altering substances, and many other events or experiences which are or may be linked with the building and sustaining of mature adult relationships can act as triggers. So can many other aspects of adult life, such as any interview situation in which there is an appraisal of the interviewee by people with authority and perceived power. Job interviews, interviews with the bank manager, benefits interviews and police interviews can be triggers to traumatic stress, plunging the sufferer into the overwhelming sensory experience of wordless terror.

In childhood the families or carers can become the carriers of the trauma for the child, entering a sort of secondary victimisation (see Kinchin, 1998, p12) as they experience in their own persons the absent feelings relating to the intense but unformed somatic energy changes in the primary victim, the child. As an adult, this secondary victimisation often moves on to the partner of the primary victim, and I have seen partners exhibiting exaggerated startle responses, tearfulness, depression, morbid thoughts, memory disturbances, uncharacteristic aggression and a range of other symptoms previously absent from their experience and apparently linked to their close relationship with the primary victim.

Victims of paedophilia commonly believe that they carry within their body a spreading poison which will damage and ultimately destroy everything it touches, or that they are, or carry within them, an explosive device (possibly implanted by the abuser) which is life threatening to anyone who loves them. The phenomenon of secondary victimisation feeds into this cognitive and affective distortion. Sufferers from this sort of childhood post traumatic stress disorder frequently receive confirmation from their environment as children and as adults that they are a source of poison in the world, and a danger to anyone who gets too close to them.

Children integrate new information about the world through play. Where adults integrate trauma through telling the story, transferring the stored fragments of sensory experience of trauma into narrative memory, children integrate new experiences through repetition of the experience in the form of play. In victims of paedophile abuse this often takes the form of compulsive re-enactment of the trauma; the intrusive recollection may never reach language at all, but manifest itself as repetitive playing out of elements of the experience.

Such re-enactment of abuse may be symbolic or literal, solitary or involving others in the 'game', but is always likely to be socially unacceptable. The child who masturbates in public, who draws other children into age-inappropriate sex games far beyond ordinary exploratory play, who sexually touches visiting adults, flirts seductively with the next door neighbour, and absent-mindedly imitates the sounds of orgasm while playing with their toy cars is unlikely to be at the top of anyone's birthday party list.

Social exclusion is only the outward expression of an even more damaging level of social unacceptability. Families and carers struggle, often at great personal cost, to relate to children whose personal, cognitive and social development have been distorted by paedophile abuse. If you live with a child who touches you inappropriately, who undresses you with their eyes, who randomly flinches or clings desperately when you touch them, who tries to kiss you open-mouthed, you are likely to begin to feel disorientated. Relating socially in a living environment to children who have been taught to relate to adults sexually contributes to the secondary victimisation of those nearest and dearest to the victim.

A further disruption of the lives of those who live with primary victims occurs at the level of assimilating at an unconscious level just what it is that paedophiles do to children. The internal inhibitors against even considering children as sexual objects are powerful. If we live with children who have been used in this way, their behaviour will show us what they cannot tell us. At that point, either our internal inhibitors must begin to break down to enable us to recognise what is happening, or the child must be consigned to oblivion as crazy. We know which way that has been resolved for most of the last century. Now we are beginning to understand why, for the pain of allowing ourselves to think the unthinkable, to accept in our daily lives that the unacceptable has happened, can be intense.

Many adults simply cannot tolerate the thoughts and images generated by accepting the message of the child's behaviour. Instead the behaviour itself becomes the focus of attention and the child acquires any one or more of a range of labels which pretend to be diagnostic but actually are no more than different ways of describing the behaviour of a child in distress.

Autonomic hyperarousal

Children who have suffered traumatic stress of this nature and degree are alert and jumpy to the point of exhausting those around them. On the other hand, the perpetual arousal to threat leads to an inability to make realistic assessments of actual risk, so that carers must substitute for the missing awareness of danger.

The heavy load of self-generated painkillers, endogenous opioids, commonly carried by victims of post traumatic stress disorder can result in children being unaware of pain, or unable to distinguish degrees of pain. Unable to make accurate assessments of risk or of pain, children are vulnerable to injury in many everyday situations, and are always likely to be the casualties in any playground game or childish adventure.

Like any other opiates, endogenous opioids can be addictive. Children can become hooked on all the chemicals generated by traumatic stress, and the addiction can be one of the causes of behaviour which causes the child to be retraumatised; addiction to self-generated opioids in particular may lead to such otherwise bizarre and inexplicable behaviours as non-suicidal self-harm, which may involve cutting, scratching, biting, piercing or carving patterns on the body.

In circumstances of extreme threat our sensory interface with the world alters. Peripheral vision, for example, becomes sharper to pick up danger signals from the widest possible visual field, whilst the capacity to focus on a narrow visual task such as reading this page is diminished. Post traumatic stress disorder includes a more or less permanent state of alertness to extreme threat, known as hypervigilance, and the capacity to perform many ordinary tasks is reduced as a result, as the sensory information which allows us to interact with our environment is altered or lost. Since the child who has suffered abuse is also likely to display wary watchfulness, continuously scanning the adults around them for non-verbal signals of readiness to abuse, there is little wonder that traumatised children are often seen as inattentive or scatterbrained.

The child suffering autonomic hyperarousal will be hyperactive as well as inattentive. It is likely that some children at least who are diagnosed as suffering from Attention Deficit Hyperactivity Disorder (ADHD) or related syndromes are also, or actually, suffering from post traumatic stress disorder. There are also specific learning difficulties associated with the alteration in perceptual fields caused by the hyper-arousal of the autonomic nervous system. Children may struggle with such tasks as reading, writing, or making sense of maps and dia-grams, and the educational underachievement which is likely to follow will further feed into the sense of unworthiness which is characteristic of abused children.

Normal brain rhythms are disturbed by the presence of stress hor-mones at these levels, and the ultradian rhythms of relaxation and sleep are often seriously disrupted. You can tell a foster carer by the bags beneath his eyes! Children deprived of normal relaxation patterns will crave the experience of altered brain waves, and in older children self-medication with mind altering substances is a common response, not only to escape the terrors of post traumatic stress disorder, but also to experience something like the altered states of consciousness which for non-traumatised people are an ordinary part of the rhythm of life.

Adults subject to hyperarousal of the autonomic nervous system enter a survival mode which provides maximum opportunity for fight or flight. Children, by contrast, are dependent on adults for their survival, so the survival system functions differently. Children commonly regress to behaviours characteristic of earlier developmental stages. Bedwetting, thumb sucking, whining and clinging, reverting to babble or infantile talk patterns, needing to be fed or, in older children, to have special symbolic foods prepared by the primary carer, needing bedtime rituals to be established or re-established, and so on. Children may smear faeces, wet or soil themselves, hide menstrual products, and in every possible way regress to a more dependent stage of childhood.

Just as there are stages in childhood development in which children believe that they are omnipotent, or are magically able to control the world around them, steps on the road to developing a sense of res-ponsibility and moral efficacy, so these processes will become dis-torted for the child suffering post traumatic stress disorder. Children who are victims often believe that they are able to predict or control future events, or that they are responsible for the safety of others, often other family members, who can only remain safe if the child remains alert. This serves both to explain and to justify the chronic hypervigilance which will not allow the child rest or respite. The linking of childhood magical thinking or illusions of omnipotence can extend to a whole range of 'superstitious' beliefs and behaviours which the child believes keep the world safe and the sun and moon and stars revolving in their orbits.

Children in this situation can become extremely dominating. Believing that they are in fact controlling the fate of the family, and that they must do so to maintain safety, they seize power at every opportunity. Where others in the family are suffering secondary victimisation and feeling weak and ineffective this can be a recipe for disaster, with everyone unknowingly contributing to an untenable and unstable family dynamic. As children move into adolescence and develop physical strength such family dysfunction can move from being uncomfortable to being dangerous, as the child desperately seeks to maintain dominance to protect the family from unnamed and unnameable disaster and destruction.

The four-year-old refugee from genocide separated from his family who a year on must still perform six bedtime rituals each night or 'something bad' will happen to his mother serves as a case in point. The fourteen-year-old survivor of a child pornography ring six years earlier who lies in bed all day because his mother is afraid he will beat her again if she tries to get him to go to school is another. Both children communicate vividly the impact in the present of the trauma in the past, as they struggle to establish control over an uncertain and terrifying world, and dominance over those around them. And we might fleetingly wonder what lay behind the behaviour of 'James James Morrison Morrison Weatherby George Dupree' in the poem by A. A. Milne, who

> Took great
> Care of his mother,
> Though he was only three.
> James James
> Said to his mother,
> 'Mother' he said, said he;
> 'You must never go down
>   to the end of the town
>   if you don't go down with me.'

The impact on the family of the traumatised child displaying such dominating and controlling behaviour, the family who may already be struggling with issues of guilt and responsibility, can be over-whelming. This can develop into yet another facet of the secondary victimisation which afflicts the kin networks of survivors of paedo-phile abuse. In adult life, the need of the survivor to control and dominate and exercise 'magical' powers over the lives of those they love can have a drastic effect on the capacity to make and sustain last-ing relationships. And where such relationships are formed, they can lead to secondary victimisation of the partner and any additions to the new family unit.

Young children with exaggerated startle responses and disturbed sleep patterns may dominate family life in quite a different way. I have been into households where adults creep around like mice through the evening, and jump to any sound, because they are afraid to wake the child, finally sleeping, and begin again the nightly battle of trying to establish peace and order whilst living with a child suffering auto-nomic hyperarousal. The result is anything but peaceful or orderly, as the activities of the rest of the household revolve around the disturbed sleeping patterns of the child.

In adolescence the child is likely to discover ways to self-medicate for the symptoms of hyperarousal, and the anxiety and stress of living with a child who is exploring substance abuse as a way to achieve some con-trol, however tenuous, over their own physiology, can further contri-bute to the secondary victimisation of parents and families of the child who is the primary victim.

Avoidance of trigger stimuli

Avoidance and denial are close kin. Invisible shapers of our lives, we who are autonomous and free rarely notice the negatives which govern our most positive choices and declarations. Those who suffer from post traumatic stress disorder do not have the luxury of being able to deny avoidance, though they may, of course, fiercely deny the origin of the complicated maze which their own mind creates out of each living day.

There are several layers of avoidance. Most obviously, victims will avoid reminders of the original trauma. This occurs entirely at an unconscious level, as it must do to be effective in protecting from harm. If the sufferer were able to think 'I'd better not do that, it might remind me of the trauma' they would already have been reminded. So avoidance works at a pre-rational level, and then, being the rational humans we are, we make sense of the choices we have made.

For most of us most of the time these invisible shapers, though power-ful, are trivial. It does not matter that some of our 'preferences' are the result of our minds protecting us from reminders of an unpleasant event. After a serious road accident many years ago when I was hit from behind whilst negotiating another vehicle on a single track road, I would go out of my way to make journeys which did not include such narrow roads. In my corner of rural Gloucestershire this was quite an exercise, and the 'reasons' I adduced for my chosen routes being 'better' were as tortuous as the roads I was avoiding. Only when finally I could not avoid a certain narrow road and felt the fear as I waited for the crash from behind did I begin to recognise what was happening.

For victims of post traumatic stress disorder this process is much more destructive of the quality of life. The intensity of the traumatic stress and the course of the developing disorder will mean that the first level of protection from direct reminders will be likely to move on to a second level of possible reminders, thus beginning the generalisa-tion of the phobic response. Someone who drove off a bridge may become unable to drive across that bridge again, which is the first level response. They may then become unable to drive over any bridges, or to walk over bridges, or to be above water in a boat, or to be within hearing of running water, by which time they have reached a disabling stage of avoidant response.

There is a third level of avoidance in post traumatic stress disorder. The disorder produces an increasing responsiveness to neutral stimuli, as the kindling of the limbic system leads to objectively safe situations or events eliciting the response of traumatic stress. Since there may be traumatic amnesia for the original event, the sufferer may then become phobic in response to the situation or event within which the hidden trigger was embedded. A child may stand in a super-market queue behind someone who smells reminiscent of the person who abused them. Without that tenuous but powerful link to the trauma ever reaching consciousness, the child may experience a terrifying panic attack, and afterwards be phobic in response to super-markets, or queues, or both.

Finally, as the disorder develops, the victim may reach the point of being effectively retraumatised by their own thoughts, as intrusive fragments of trauma memory replay obsessively in the imagination. Avoidance then can only be achieved by extreme measures. The use of mind-altering substances may keep the terrifying thoughts at bay. Various sorts of obsessive behaviour can be temporarily effective, focusing the mind for a time on something other than the intensifying cycle of intrusion and avoidance of horrifying, often formless and nameless, thoughts. Sports, games, computer activities, puzzles, sexual behaviour, reading, shopping, cleaning, any activity which can serve to occupy the mind for a time may be tried. These may be out-wardly the same activities which for others are creative, constructive, or relaxing ways to spend time; they will be distinguished as avoidance activities by the compulsive, addictive, joyless manner in which they take over the lives of victims. There may also be times when the only way to avoid the unspeakable horror of intrusive thoughts is to replace them with other horrific thoughts which feel more within the victim's control. Then suicidal thoughts take over, and plans for ways to end the suffering become the only remaining recourse of a mind lost in the maze it generated to protect itself.

Avoidant children may absent themselves from certain lessons at school, or they may absent themselves from school altogether. They may vehemently dislike particular foods or drinks, disappearing from the scene when just not eating or not drinking at a shared meal would be noticeable and seem odd. They may be unable to undress in front of others, and always fall ill on days when sports or swimming are included on the agenda.

Children who have survived or who are surviving paedophile abuse may present further problems for schools. They may disappear at break times, or at lesson times, or at meal times, or at assembly times, hiding themselves away for a while, or taking themselves off to somewhere which feels safer to them. The disappearance may be an inward withdrawal from contact rather than a physical removal from the potentially threatening scene. Every teacher knows the child who may be present in body, but is emphatically absent in spirit. Distraction activities may also be effective for the child in avoiding a panic attack, and teachers who are trying to contain a child who so passionately needs to disrupt the lesson can throw away their lesson plans however many hours they spent on them.

The need to rationalise the avoidant behaviour is pressing. For the child to acknowledge the avoidance would negate the effectiveness of the defence mechanism, confronting the child with the reality of the underlying trauma spilling over from the past into the present. Although this would be part of a healing process, that would only be in the context of the child having learned to modulate the intense arousal. In the context of untreated post traumatic stress disorder the child needs to deny the avoidance where possible. It is easy for children in this situation to accept a label of 'disruptive' , which at least feels powerful, rather than venture one step into the territory of fear and panic which may be the starting point for the unacceptable behaviour. Children are all too willing to collude with adults in defining themselves as unacceptable, disruptive, antisocial, a definition which in any case feeds into and confirms the eroded sense of self-worth which is another legacy of childhood trauma.

For the secondary victims, the kin and carers, the avoidant child may be literally and metaphorically a nightmare to live with. Avoidance is successful as a psychological defence insofar as it enables the child to not-experience the fear and terror of the trauma which is being avoided. The effects of living with children who are not-feeling the terror which dominates and defines their lives are extraordinarily powerful. Surrounded by invisible and unspeakable horrors which cannot be acknowledged, for they exist in the here-and-now only in the mind of the one person who cannot possibly recognise their existence, carers can find themselves becoming inexplicably symptomatic.

They may develop generalised anxieties, nightmares, sleep disturbances and physical symptoms such as breathing problems or digestive disturbances. It is as though they were feeling the fear for the child, who, unable to tolerate or acknowledge the terror, avoids and displaces it. Others, with less commitment to the child, are likely to opt out of relating to the child, finding it uncomfortable to do so and simply avoiding that discomfort without ever bringing into consciousness its source. Children may be progressively excluded from social contact by people who simply find them unpleasant company; again, this will feed into the erosion of self-worth and social acceptability which is itself a product of abuse.

Those who cannot so easily escape the company of the disturbing child, who are tied in by bonds of commitment and responsibility, will find themselves living with the disturbance of their own feelings as well as the disruptions of the child's behaviour. Close kin who may carry their own burdens of guilt and distress for their failure to protect the child, even where such protection may have been impossible to provide or understandably lacking, are additionally vulnerable to experiencing disturbed thoughts and feelings in relation to the child.

Numbing of responsiveness

Traumatic stress closes down many ordinary functions of the human organism. Under the impact of trauma our brain, nerves, muscles, glands, heart, lungs, liver, stomach, bowels, bladder, sexual organs, and skin all function differently. In post traumatic stress disorder these changes are extended into ordinary life as though the trauma were still occurring or being repeated.

This is bad news for the victim. The responses of traumatic stress are emergency responses. They will promote to the maximum the chances of surviving a horrific event. Confronted with a hungry sabre-toothed tiger the child of our primitive ancestors most likely to survive was presumably the child who produced the responses we now recognise as traumatic stress. In that situation a dependent child needs to be able to freeze ordinary functioning, switch off language which slows up the brain and nervous system, achieve maximum pain endurance, and engage adults as rescuers by regressing to infantile behaviours. Whoever could do all that instantly and without conscious effort was the child most likely to live to become our one-generation-less-primitive ancestor. These responses become seriously dysfunctional when extended into everyday living.

The child is physically primed to exert maximum effort and to feel minimum pain, is deprived of normal sensory awareness of the here-and-now environment, and may have reverted to an infantile level of functioning for parts of their behaviour. Children become physically uncoordinated, clumsy and accident prone. They may fail to notice injuries, or be unable to indicate accurately the site of pain. I have walked miles with a child who needed to expend some energy, only to discover at the end of the walk that on the beach that morning, hours earlier, a large triangular piece of glass had become embedded in her foot. She gave no indication of having suffered any pain, and only began to limp while climbing a tower for the view. On another occasion, having learned better awareness, I have accurately diagnosed earache in a child presenting with a sore knee!

The numbing of responsiveness is emotional as well as physical. Constantly beset by an inchoate jumble of somatic sensations which are the nearest approach to feelings for the child victim of post traumatic stress disorder, children find it impossible to discern in themselves the shades of emotional fluctuation which they can see in others. At the moment of trauma, emotions are a luxury the victim will do better without. When that moment is extended to become all moments, the victim is left with an impoverished and stunted life. Liking and disliking, curiosity, playfulness, delight and joy are all lost. When joy is lost from life, each day becomes an obstacle course to be survived, never an adventure to be seized with delight.

Even more soul-destroying for those closest to the primary victim is the numbing of social responsiveness which goes with post traumatic stress disorder. Shotter (1984) proposes that childhood development is about the development of the self through the learning of 'social accountability', a process in which the growing child becomes increasingly able to take responsibility for themselves and their own actions, as those actions are reflected back to them by the people who love them. A key element in this process is the recognition that intentions and not just actions are crucial to human social interaction: 'Personal relationships need to be described in a way exclusively human;

in terms of what the people involved in them are trying to do.' (Shotter, 1984, p.54).

The child who is a victim of post traumatic stress disorder is trying to survive. This supersedes all other intentionality. The significant loss of the capacity for social intentionality places an insuperable barrier between the child and the rest of the world, a barrier which can be heartbreaking for those closest to the child. There is a sense of a glass wall around the child: we can see that they are there, but we cannot 'get through to them', cannot establish the give and take of social interaction, the mutually delightful exploration of being in the world together which is the mark and measure of a human relationship.

Intense emotional reactions

Having accepted that children exhibit a numbing of physical, emotional and social responsiveness when suffering from post traumatic stress disorder, it must also be recognised that they are likely to exhibit an intensification of emotional reactiveness. The combination of autonomic hyperarousal and numbness to social interaction leads to a hair-trigger reactiveness to objectively neutral social stimuli: 'Traumatised people go immediately from stimulus to res - ponse without being able to figure out what makes them so upset' (van der Kolk, McFarlane and van der Hart in van der Kolk *et al*, 1996, p422).

The reaction is characteristically one of either intense fear, a panic attack, or intense rage, sometimes called a 'limbic storm rage', in which an adult or older child lashes out with the uncontrolled frenzy of a toddler having a tantrum. Or both fear and rage may be experienced, either simultaneously or successively.

The intense reactions of the traumatised child are disabling for the child and potentially dangerous for everyone involved. The levels of disorder which I have seen in children who have been victims of paedophile abuse have led to serious questions about safety and dangerousness. Children may also become terrified of the anger within them, frequently using words like exploding, unexploded bomb, and erupting volcano, to describe themselves.

When the disorder persists into adult life there may sometimes be even more serious consequences. In 1995 Bob Johnson wrote of his work with convicted murderers:

> 'When the two six-year-olds stopped jumping up and down on their five-year-old school mate they expected her to get up and run off like their favourite cartoon characters. She couldn't. She was dead. This actually occurred in a Scandinavian infants' school – and sadly nowadays, it could happen anywhere. Unless we learn from this modern parable, it will haunt us indefinitely.
>
> It is easy to lose the thread – either in recriminations ... or in hand-wringing as to our 'evil nature'. The truth is more mundane, child murderers are un-common, but lethal infantile rage is commonplace.
>
> Every one of the fifty or so murderers whom I now know well confirms that their violent destructive act emanated from a stunted child within, throwing a tantrum. Indeed, I now go further, concluding that all violence is infantile.
>
> From an article in The Guardian, 13 September 1995

Bob Johnson's work in Parkhurst prison seems to have been outstand-ingly successful in reducing incidents of violence, reducing the need for tranquillising medication, and increasing prosocial behaviour among prisoners on the unit. Unfortunately the success depended on establishing and maintaining a belief that even the most violent of people would wish to be sociable if they could, and that learning to be as sociable as they would like to be means unlearning behaviour patterns generated by childhood trauma. This did not fit well with the then current ideas about crime and violent criminals, and the work was stopped.

Yet intense emotional reactions, including precisely the sort of panic attacks and violent rages described by the men with whom Johnson worked, are known to be a symptom of post traumatic stress disorder. We might reasonably wonder just how much violence could be re-duced or eradicated in our society if we took seriously the task of pro-moting healing and recovery for traumatised children.

Without that sort of commitment from the rest of society, those who live with and care for the victims of paedophile abuse will continue to experience the secondary victimisation inevitable among those who live with actual or potential uncontrollable violence on a daily basis.

Learning difficulties

People whose brains are partly switched off are unlikely to be able to learn easily. It is therefore no surprise to discover that victims of post traumatic stress disorder suffer a variety of learning difficulties.

This is true for adults, who often cease to be able to make sense of simple propositions, or to make the sort of connections between disparate bits of information which is at the heart of much learning, or who find that the disturbances of memory associated with post traumatic stress disorder make it impossible to retain information and skills.

It is predictably much more marked in children who have suffered sexual abuse. The combination of impaired language skills, impaired short-term memory, altered sensory functioning, hypervigilance, poor concentration, preoccupation with trauma-related affect, and poor social functioning, all directly attributable to the effects of post traumatic stress disorder, make it remarkable that child victims can learn at all.

Yet they do learn. And since human beings are endlessly inventive and creative in the ways they find to manage their lives and make the best play they can with the hands dealt to them, some of them do very well at school. Which does not mean they did not have learning difficulties as a result of the trauma, but only that for them it was possible to pack up the worst effects into a different corner of their lives and find in the school environment a safer space to explore.

It is exceptionally difficult for victims of post traumatic stress disorder to learn through standard approaches to behaviour modification. The fragmented self can produce half a dozen different responses to the same stimulus in as many hours (minutes, it seems sometimes!), and ideas of rewards and punishments become meaningless as the child struggles to discover any semblance of inner consensus about what is happening to them.

Our social structures for the teaching and learning of behaviour are deeply based on the concept of punishment. Yet those most likely to produce antisocial behaviour, victims of childhood trauma, are those least likely to learn from a system based on punishment. Consider the blocks which may prevent the child from learning:

- they may have acted as they did while in a dissociated state, in which case they will not know what they have done; the punishment will be meaningless

- they may have acted as they did because they had been triggered to trauma and suffered an intense emotional reaction which was beyond their control; the punishment will be ineffective

- they may have acted as they did because their behaviour fulfilled some trauma-related personal construct such as 'I am an evil person who does terrible things'; the punishment will reinforce the distorted self-concept and actually increase the likelihood that the behaviour will be repeated

- they may have acted as they did because the social isolation of post traumatic stress disorder has prevented them from ever learning more prosocial behaviour; the punishment will provide no model for prosocial learning, but will be just another small trauma in a traumatised life.

Those who live with the victims of post traumatic stress disorder will struggle endlessly with the puzzle of how to carry on a daily life with people who seem incapable of learning many simple things, while being obviously able and competent in other areas. I have seen families driven to distraction as the normal processes of learning through which we make our lives together all fail dismally.

Instead of the expectations we normally have of childhood learning in which the assumption tends to be that adults teach and children learn, we have to accept a situation in which the child can learn nothing from us until we have learned to navigate the spaces in which they live. I once described the process to a child in my care as being like 'trying to dance with someone when only they can hear the music, and every time you think you are learning the steps they change the record.' For in the end, since the child cannot learn some things, we must learn how to teach them better.

Memory disturbance

Changes in brain function lead to a range of disturbances of memory. Children commonly suffer amnesia for the traumatic event, or for parts of the event. They may be able to remember isolated fragments of the trauma, or those fragments may be present but have a different quality from ordinary memories, so that they may seem like dreams, nightmares or images from films. All of which makes it very difficult for investigators to gain any accurate picture of crimes which it is clear have been committed, nearly all of the activities associated with paedophilia being criminal acts in this country, but which may never be proved.

These are spontaneous memory losses associated with trauma. Children who have been victims of paedophile abuse may also have been fuddled with alcohol or drugs, or have been confused by the intentionally mystifying language and behaviour of the abusers, or have been abused in circumstances or surroundings which are designed to confuse and muddle the vulnerable child.

Sometimes children become quite desperate in their attempts to 'dislodge' memories which they can sense exist, which they feel are of great importance to them, but which they cannot bring to the surface. I have seen children hitting themselves on the head, and when asked why explaining that 'it's just in here' as they point to a spot on their head just behind their ear, 'I know it is there, but I can't get to it.'

Children may also suffer hypermnesia for the trauma, a condition in which the child cannot forget the trauma or, more often, isolated memory fragments of it. These traumatic memories obsessively replay over and over again in the inner world of the victim, making it impossible to concentrate on external events. This constant re-experiencing of the trauma sustains the kindling of the limbic system, so that the child is progressively retraumatised by their own memories. Sometimes the fragments of memory favour one sensory channel over the others, so that a child may be said to be hearing voices, when the voices are in fact the memories of the voices of the abusers, or a child seeing visual hallucinations of traumatic memories may be said to be always daydreaming, especially if the visual memories are divorced from affect, so not causing immediate agitation in the behaviour of the child.

Post traumatic stress disorder also leads to loss of short term memory. Children who suffer this symptom are infinitely frustrating to live with, as they stand aimlessly at the top of the stairs having forgotten on the journey why you asked them to go up there, or three times in three days forget to bring home the letter about the school trip they so desperately want to join. Then they cover their tracks. They can see that they have a problem here not shared by their friends, so they bluff or fabricate. They invent wild stories to explain why they do not have whatever it is they have forgotten. They pretend to be wilfully disobedient or uncooperative, since it is better to be naughty than to be crazy.

Sometimes the short-term memory is not absent, but is distorted by the irregular perceptual fields which are characteristic of children who suffer post traumatic stress disorder, as hypervigilance changes the way the world can be perceived. Then it can be intriguing patiently to offer reminders of the experience you are trying to recall to memory, to see what finally causes the memories to mesh.

I recall once going with a child to visit someone who was disabled and used an electric wheelchair, and who lived in a most unusual house adapted in many striking ways to accommodate his disability. Nothing would remind the child next day of the visit we had made. Eventually I made a story of the visit, and began a painstaking description of the geography of the living room. As I reached the small table by the window the child's face lit up, 'Oh, you mean the house with the green glass ashtrays' he said with evident delight. Once anchored and accessed, the memory returned intact as a very clear visual image of the entire house as we had seen it.

Memory loss of this type and scale is another aspect of post traumatic stress disorder which feels to the sufferer and those who care for them like craziness. It is not normal for children to have such poor memories, and families have often told me so. Agonising over the child who seems at least one sandwich short of a picnic, it can be all too easy for families to collude with the child's need to define themselves as bad when the only alternative seems to be to accept that they are mad.

Dissociation

Patients who have learned to dissociate in response to trauma are likely to continue to utilize dissociative defences when exposed to new stresses. They develop amnesia for some experiences, and tend to react with fight-or-flight responses to feeling threatened, none of which may be consciously remembered afterwards. People who suffer from dissociative disorders are a clinical challenge, particularly in regard to helping them acquire a sense of personal responsibility for their actions and reactions; forensically, they are a nightmare. (van der Kolk, McFarlane and van der Hart in van der Kolk et al, 1996, p423)

Children pretend passionately. What we from our condescending height call play, they call being. Trauma cuts across the ceaseless flux of exploration and experiment like a surgeon's knife cutting into living flesh. Children are more likely than adults to dissociate at the point of trauma, for it is an effective defence against extreme terror which is already part of their otherwise rather empty psychological toolkit. They don't know how to save themselves from harm, for they are too young and inexperienced, but they do know how to play 'let's pretend'.

Paedophile abuse of every kind is particularly likely to generate a dissociative defensive response, since it is always such a gross assault on the integrity of the person. Children who save themselves from destruction at the point of abuse by doing what developmentally they know how to do and becoming someone else, are particularly vulnerable to dissociative disorders. And children who suffer from dissociative disorders are not only a forensic nightmare, though they are certainly that, but are also terribly difficult to live with on a daily basis.

Consider this vignette, a common one in schools: Robert kicks Rebecca (hard!), the teacher sees him do it. 'You kicked Rebecca! That was very naughty'. 'No, Miss, it wasn't me'. The child is clearly lying. Yet the teacher is confused, for all the non-verbal indicators suggest complete sincerity. Here is a child who seems to believe passionately what every external observer can testify is not the case. This is a very general story, but I have in mind a particular example, with an unusual ending. Perceptive teacher asks a sensible question to clear up her own confusion: 'Who did do it then?' and Robert answers 'It wasn't me, Miss. Robert did it.'

Try living for a while with a child who is not one person but two, or three, or six people. Try getting up in the morning never knowing which child you will meet at the breakfast table. Will it be the bubbly extrovert without a care in the world, and with the concentration span of a butterfly, or will it be the suicidal depressive who, if persuaded to eat at all, will probably weep silently into their cornflakes, or perhaps it will be the bear-with-a-sore-head-on-a-short-fuse who might just upend the entire breakfast table before storming out to school?

The links to normal childhood and adolescent behaviour are clear. Most children try on different personalities for size, most teenagers are unpredictable as they struggle to gain control over their rampant hormones and establish themselves in the world. But the child who dissociates in response to stress is so extreme, so unpredictable, so gravely disordered in their parody of ordinary growing up, that families become disorientated and are driven to despair. And the more serious the precipitating trauma, the less serious the stressor need be which will provide the proximate cause for the dissociative response.

Children who have been victims of paedophile abuse may react with dissociation to almost any stress. In these different states they may call themselves by different names, like different foods, dress differently, walk differently, and have entirely different sets of memories.

In adulthood they are likely to present their partners with a bewildering array of different relationships, when the partner had thought they were relating to the one beloved other, and to be impervious to the confusion and fear they are arousing by their disordered behaviour, interpreting any expression of pain and distress from their bewildered partner as a statement of rejection.

Bewildered, confused, and probably frightened as well, those who live closely with primary victims of trauma who suffer dissociative disorders are very likely to become secondary victims, suffering more or less severe impairment of personal and social functioning.

Aggression against self and others

Children who are physiologically primed to fight are going to have to do something with that energy, will need to find some discharge for the tension in those long muscles. The arms and legs and shoulders and neck and jaw ache with the need to punch and kick and wrestle and tear and bite. Somebody somewhere is going to get hurt.

Often it is the victims themselves. The perpetrator of abuse is a very powerful person in the life of the child. Children begin to accumulate personal power, the ability to be effective in the world, as they internalize the powerful figures in their lives. It is therefore natural for children to internalize the aggressor to reduce the crushing powerlessness of their situation as victim. The internalised aggressor can then continue to victimize the child even when the actual perpetrator is safely tucked up in his or her own bed dreaming the dreams of an untroubled mind.

Sometimes the child may reach a sustainable equilibrium by entirely taking on the role of the aggressor, and becoming a perpetrator of abuse themselves. This seems to be a relatively rare response; estimates vary, but generally agree that it is a small minority of sexually abused children who go on to become perpetrators of sexual abuse against children.

The majority use their capacity to split into different selves to provide the internalised aggressor with the perfect victim. They harm themselves, thus potentially killing several birds with one stone, as they discharge the muscular tension of long muscles primed for aggression, act out the two roles most central in their lives, aggressor and victim, possibly generate a burst of endogenous opioids as they suffer the pain, and confirm the predictability of a world in which pain and suffering are the threads which hold the fabric together.

Most of the self-harm which follows sexual abuse is to do with pain and suffering rather than suicide. Sometimes the aggression against the self will extend to wishing to kill. It is not uncommon for victims of paedophile abuse to feel suicidal, and some of them do kill themselves. The suicidal impulses seem to spring from various states of mind following the abuse. Depression and despair may lead to wanting to end a life which does not seem worth living. Recognising that the pain of life as a victim is not going to go away, can lead to a perspective in which the sum of pain if life goes on seems too much to bear. A sense of unworthiness, or of being a contaminating influence on the lives of beloved others, can make it seem necessary to destroy the source of the contamination. And sometimes the pent-up aggression can lead to a sort of self-murder, an act of spontaneous murderous rage turned against the self.

Sooner or later other people will be hurt as well, not necessarily abusively, with the child in the role of perpetrator, but with a sort of grim statistical inevitability. If someone feels that murderous that often, if they feel this terrified on this many occasions, if they are subject to intense and unpredictable emotional reactions this many times a day or week or month, then eventually they will hurt someone else.

Families and other carers can find this very frightening. Since the primary victim is invariably frightened of the violence they feel within, these fears will feed one another, and the situation can become dangerously explosive. I have seen families who have lurched from violent incident to violent incident for years, feeling shamed and stigmatised that they cannot manage their child, hiding bruises and desperately clinging to the belief that this time the child will keep their promises and never get into such a rage again. The stage is then set for the development of a lifetime of domestic violence, and the circles of secondary victimisation widen.

Some drug use among victims of post traumatic stress disorder seems to be an attempt to manage rage which all other efforts have failed to control. Heroin users in particular who have a history of traumatic stress commonly relate their use of heroin to attempts to manage anger. This may be successful for a time, but is unlikely to be effective as a long-term strategy for self-management. It also leads to further fears and stresses for the families and carers.

Psychosomatic disorders

Stress hormones at the level found in victims of post traumatic stress disorder can wreak havoc with many physical functions. All the major organs, glands and muscle groups are affected. Extended over years this can lead to a host of illnesses and physical problems including digestive disorders, breathing problems, sexual dysfunction, back ache, headaches, and disorders of the immune system which is put under considerable strain by the perpetual state of emergency which is PTSD.

Sufferers also commonly have an impoverished or absent ability to put feelings into words, but instead experience the changes of energy associated with feelings as somatic states. Having no language or symbol for such feelings as excitement, happiness, or fear, they experience indigestion or asthma or diarrhoea instead.

Children who have been victims of paedophile abuse may also have a range of health problems associated with the nature of the abuse. They may suffer sexually transmitted diseases, or have recurrent problems such as thrush. I have worked with children with chronic pain from old injuries at the time of abuse, probably caused by such practices as severe beatings and being tied up for long periods with the hands above the head. They may have been introduced by abusers to the use of addictive substances. Older children may be at a stage of being legitimately sexually active, but may have learned unhealthy sexual practices which will lead to continuing health problems. Although these are physical problems, they are generated and sustained by the body-mind disorders arising from the trauma of paedophile abuse.

There are also the health-related anxieties associated with having suffered such abuse. Children may believe that they are impure or unclean, that their genitals are disgusting, that menstruation or nocturnal emissions are some sort of punishment, or that they have some specific condition such as AIDS. These anxieties feed into the psychosomatic reactions of post traumatic stress disorder and contribute further to the undermining of the health.

> The truth about our childhood is stored up in our body, and although we can repress it, we can never alter it. Our intellect can be deceived, our feelings manipulated, our perceptions confused, and our body tricked with medication. But someday the body will present its bill, for it is as incorruptible as a child who, still whole in spirit, will accept no compromises or excuses, and it will not stop tormenting us until we stop evading the truth (Miller, 1990, p318).

Secondary victims

Those who have, or who establish, close affectional bonds with children who have been victims of paedophile abuse or adults who were victims as children are exposed to a range of experiences which can be so damaging that they produce symptoms. When we commit ourselves to a loving relationship we make ourselves vulnerable. The effects of paedophilia are highly toxic. Primary victims tell us so in very vivid terms, and professionals agree with them.

> All child abuse is grotesque – but have a care when entering this field. The emotional forces involved are so strong they distort an adult into seeing tiny infants as 'sex-objects', and they are quite strong enough to seriously injure anyone who meddles inexpertly in such toxic waters, however well intended (Bob Johnson, *The Guardian*, 28 June 1995).

Families and, later, partners can scarcely be regarded as experts. Yet they can hardly avoid 'meddling' if they are to continue living with the person they love, for day by day and hour by hour the suffering victim will be producing behaviour to which they must react and respond. Small wonder, then, that these close kin often begin to be symptomatic themselves, exhibiting emotional and behavioural changes reminiscent of the post traumatic stress disorder which afflicts the one they love.

This may be compounded by the fact that paedophiles often target families directly, wooing and seducing the protective parents into believing that their child is safe with the abuser. This is a form of direct secondary abuse which leaves family members even more likely to become secondary victims of post traumatic stress disorder. The complex realisations and negotiations which must take place in order to ensure the safety of the child once the abuse is recognised often destroy at a stroke all the fragile structures of respect and trust which lie at the heart of functioning families. Then family members have nowhere to go but into the vortex of trauma, where assumptions are shattered and meaning collapses.

Foster carers are also not 'expert' in the sense used by Bob Johnson, nor are most residential child care staff. These people are highly vulnerable as they provide the service they are there to offer, and in so doing find themselves cast headlong into the 'toxic waters' of paedophile abuse, and many secondary victims may be found among those who have taken responsibility on behalf of the rest of the community for the day to day care of traumatised children.

Secondary victimisation has received very little attention, even in areas where there has been heightened awareness of the stress suffered by carers. It is a field which urgently needs further study, for it is impossible for us to provide adequate care and safety for children who are victims of paedophile abuse if we do not recognise the needs of the carers. And it is difficult for adults who were abused as children to establish and maintain satisfying relationships in adult life in a community which has no understanding of the experiences of partners and children, the people who even at that remove from the original abuse may become victims as they live close to the disordered behaviour and emotions of the primary victim.

It will also become clear, I think, that expertise is not a certain shield against the toxicity of paedophilia. There are social, political and organisational pressures which operate in this field. When these are added to the personal stresses of staying sane and rational and happy while working professionally in the field of paedophile abuse, even the most expert practitioner may find themselves becoming symptomatic (see B. Hudnall Stamm, 1995). I have found an uncomfortably high casualty rate amongst workers in the field of paedophilia, a tertiary victimisation which can affect almost anyone, however experienced and whatever their level of qualification.

> Continuing ignorance of the scale of abuse, combined with an inability to negotiate the difficulty and complexity of this area, means that it is impossible to plan for it organisationally, emotionally and professionally. This means that we will continue to be both reactive and uncoordinated. This is exacerbated by the skill and cunning employed by child abusers to perpetuate their crimes (Catherine Doran and Chris Brannan in Bibby, 1996, p157).

So long as it remains 'impossible' to make organisational, emotional and professional plans to deal with organised abuse, paedophilia will continue to create traumatic stress for the professionals who must confront it, and some of them will become tertiary victims.

Chapter 6

Traumatic stress in adults
the shattering of assumptions

For every static world that you or I impose
Upon the real one must crack at times and new
Patterns from new disorders open like a rose
And old assumptions yield to new sensation;
The Stranger in the wings is waiting for his cue,
The fuse is always laid to some annunciation.
'Mutations', Louis MacNeice

It seems that adults who have not themselves suffered the trauma of paedophilia, and who are not kin to children who are victims of paedophile abuse, can become victims of post traumatic stress disorder through their professional involvement in work which requires them to engage with this subject.

This is not stress, which is a familiar companion of the professional tasks undertaken by these workers. It is the development of symptoms of post traumatic stress disorder, the disabling terror which affects every aspect of life with its characteristic indicators of intrusion, avoidance and autonomic hyperarousal. It is characteristic of the disorder that in a population exposed to trauma, some people will remain free of symptoms, some will develop symptoms over the following weeks and months, and some will remain severely affected for a considerable time. It is also characteristic that of those who do develop symptoms some will suffer aspects of disorder without progressing to the full spread of disabling symptoms which would merit a diagnosis of post traumatic stress disorder, while others will go on to develop the full-blown disorder.

It is essential to remember that the people who do this work are almost always the most experienced and respected members of the workforce, who are likely to have been working for years in their high stress occupations. In both the police and social services departments, officers assigned to child protection work tend to be those who are experienced workers with a demonstrable record of stability and sound professional judgement. Foster carers entrusted with the most behaviourally disturbed children, or children known to have been subject to organised sexual abuse are usually carers of proven experience and practical expertise. Teachers who work with educationally disruptive children are usually those who have the calm and stable approach likely to be effective in managing the presenting problems. And so on. The people who find themselves plunged into the 'toxic waters' of investigating paedophilia and caring for its victims are generally mature, stable, healthy and well-adjusted individuals with tried and tested strategies for managing the stress and distress of their demanding professions.

> We are confronted with a psychological disorder that can strike psychologically healthy individuals. What is clear is that there are extreme life events that will produce psychological difficulties not in a vulnerable few, but in large numbers of people exposed to them. (Janoff-Bulman, 1992, p50).

The prevalence of psychological difficulties among the people whose stories I have heard has been extraordinary and moving. So many felt that their lives had been turned upside down, and that they had been changed forever by their experiences. Some had formal diagnoses of post traumatic stress disorder, others had experienced psychological, emotional, or physical symptoms which they attributed to the experience of working in this field, and which had from time to time interfered with their daily lives enough to need medical intervention. Some had experienced major changes in their quality and style of life, in terms of work and personal or social relationships, and again these respected and previously stable people have attributed these unsought changes to the effects of this work.

In what sense can this work be understood as trauma? Here we have a population who have nothing in common except exposure to work in the field of paedophilia, who seem to develop symptoms of post traumatic stress disorder, and who attribute their distress to the work they share. Bob Johnson is clearly right to describe this work as 'toxic', yet that is still just a description of the effects – it does not in any way explain how a field of work like this can be so damaging to those who work in it.

There are jobs and work tasks which are known to have a traumatic effect. Soldiers, sailors, pilots and others in the armed forces, fire-fighters, ambulance staff, police officers, doctors, nurses, disaster workers, anyone whose work involves body retrieval, are all workers whose employment carries a risk of exposure to traumatic stress. They will be aware at the time of enlisting or enrolling for the work that they might be called on to undertake tasks which score highly as stressors, and which we now know have a high toxicity for the development of post traumatic stress disorder. Stressors, or toxins, in this context include threat to life, exposure to death and to dead bodies, personal bereavement, loss of property, stigmatisation, injury, fatigue, disruption of normal physiological functioning through such factors as sleep deprivation, hunger, thirst, extreme heat or cold, and so on (see Ursano, Grieger and McCarroll in van der Kolk *et al*, 1996, p446).

It is in the nature of such work that some workers will be injured, and we now understand that some injuries will be caused by traumatic stress rather than, or as well as, physical injury. The now quite substantial research on such occupations and their effects on workers is leading to a growing body of knowledge about how to manage the tasks involved to minimise injuries, and how to educate and support workers to diminish vulnerability and increase resilience.

Work which involves exposure to the after-effects of paedophilia is not likely to generate more than a few of the listed toxins, and even those are likely to be far less extreme than the stressors encountered in emergency or disaster work. Yet the prevalence and intensity of symptoms I have encountered among workers in the field of organised and network child sexual abuse would suggest that such employment places workers in a high risk category for the development of post traumatic stress disorder.

If my perceptions of the effects of paedophilia are accurate, if as Bob Johnson suggests this is highly toxic work, then some factors must be adduced to account for the toxicity other than those already familiar through studies of high risk occupations. The work of Ronnie Janoff-Bulman is helpful here; in 1992 she proposed that a key to understanding the damage done by trauma is the recognition that traumatic events and circumstances can catastrophically destroy certain basic assumptions we hold about the world.

The destruction of meaning and value

The world as we know it is not the world as it is. This is a truth we need to forget often in order to function. In general we have to behave as though the assumptive world we inhabit were exactly the same as the objective world which is our environment. Except in the case of trauma, and perhaps ecstasy, sensory information reaching the thalamus is processed through the pre-frontal cortex. All our non-extreme experience of our environment is mediated to us through the specifically human, thinking, language and symbol making, part of our brains.

Thus we perceive the world as it can be fitted into the metaphors and symbols our minds create in order to allow creatures with such a complex brain to function and not to be paralysed by the sheer quantity of information impinging on us. We attribute value to some bits of the information reaching us, and screen out other bits of information as worthless to us, and we do all that, quite unconsciously, before we can start to perceive an event or think about an experience.

> In this way static patterns of value become the universe of distinguishable things. Elementary static distinctions between such entities as 'before' and 'after' and between 'like' and 'unlike' grow into enormously complex patterns of knowledge that are transmitted from generation to generation as the mythos, the culture in which we live (*Lila*, Robert M. Pirsig, 1991, p 145).

The majority of us function with adequate efficiency for most of the time. It is only when something goes wrong with our senses that we notice the possibility of a gap between the world of our assumptions and the world as it is. New lenses in our spectacles will do it, as we miss our footing when the pavement we see and the pavement that is turn out to be in different places, or coffee cups crash to the floor as the real world table does not match the position of the table we can see so clearly. Unfamiliarity may raise our awareness; after a year of seeing no television I discovered that moving patterns of light do not of themselves form recognisable images, but need interpreting, which my brain had momentarily forgotten to do.

Once we realise that even the physical world we inhabit is actually an assumptive construct, a metaphor our mind creates in order to make sense of an otherwise unmanageable quantity of information, it is much easier to grasp that the complex world of relationships and interdependencies which forms our personal and social reality is a construct based on a set of assumptions we make about the world.

Learning takes place when our assumptive world changes, when the constructs which are our map or image of reality adapt to accommodate new information. Those who learn most easily are those who have most clarity and most flexibility in the constructs which make up their inner world, the constructs which serve both as templates and as models for the environment in which they find themselves. If the clarity fades or the inner map becomes inflexibly distorted, as in some degenerative conditions of the brain, we may find people superimposing the geography of the past onto the present, and trying to walk down staircases or light fires in fireplaces, the positions of which are accurate for homes of their past but dangerously inaccurate in the present.

It will be clear that there must be some sort of hierarchy of assumptions. At the most superficial level of mapping the physical world against the evidence of our senses, there is need for as much accuracy as possible but no overwhelming emotional investment. Learning at this level tends to come relatively easily. If the outer world changes significantly or the reliability of our sensory organs alters, it is important for our survival unscathed that we adapt to those changes, but it usually does not involve intolerable emotional turmoil to make the adaptation.

It seems to be intrinsic to the human mind to make assumptions of a different order. The work of Gregory Bateson (1972, for example) was very rich in elucidating the complexity of the human capacity to create constructs which hugely increase our ability to learn by allowing us to generalise and think in categories. What has become clear is that we are compelled by the structures of our mind to create such generalisations. Not only are we able to think in abstract constructs, which is our glory, but we are unable not to do so, which can be our downfall.

As our assumptions about the world reach levels of greater abstraction and complexity they begin to take the shape of persistent cognitive constructs which allow us to organise our understanding of the world around us, constructs which represent our theories of the world at various levels, and which have been called schemas (Janoff-Bulman, 1992, p28). Schemas include both knowledge of attributes and images of relationships between the attributes; they are our maps of the world. The concept of cognitive schemas is still being developed, but does present a helpful pointer to the way our mind may process and structure information.

Some of our schemas exist at a low level of abstraction, enabling us to assign objects in the world to a category or class, and to specify objects as members of a class; we are thus provided with linguistic or symbolic shortcuts to making sense of our environment. Table is a much tidier concept than 'square wooden object with four legs which serves as a resting place for food and equipment during meals'; it also allows for much more elegance in rapidly recognising a host of other objects which may be different in size, shape, material construction, or function, but which are recognisably tables.

Other cognitive schemas represent our attempts to codify and make sense of our families, our world or the cosmos. Some of these schemas at higher levels of abstraction are the maps which encode our deepest beliefs and assumptions. They represent the meanings we assign to the world; they are the filters through which the world is mediated to us. The creation of such constructs seems to be intrinsic to the human mind. We do seem to be a meaning-making animal.

Language and other symbols are intrinsic to the metaphors by which we construct and make sense of the world. Proverbs illustrate this beautifully. These are very ancient cross-cultural schemas which can indicate to us how human beings have mapped their experience of the world for thousands of years. From simple weather proverbs of the 'red sky at night' variety, by which agricultural and fishing communities struggled to impose some predictability on an uncertain world, through to attempts to come to terms with tragedy, such as 'only the good die young'.

All schemas tend to persist; it is their nature. Although superficial level schemas may be very flexible, to allow the assimilation of new information, they would be useless if they had no persistent shape. An object must have at least some of the attributes and functions of a table for us to classify it as such. It must match our theory of tables, although it may expand the theory in new and interesting ways.

Our theories of the world must persist to allow us to function; they often do persist beyond all objective and rational expectation. The Flat Earth Society provides a magnificent example of the tenacity of 'common sense' schemas long after they have been disconfirmed, and in this case long after the 'common' sense about the world had adapted to the new information and accepted that the shape of the earth is a flattened sphere.

As a general rule, the higher the level of abstraction of the schema, the more it will persist, even in the face of disconfirming evidence. Indeed, human beings have been known to persist in their highest level abstractions, their most fundamental assumptions and beliefs, even though confronted with apparently overwhelming disconfirmation.

Our core assumptions probably arise out of our need to survive childhood. Janoff-Bulman proposes that the three fundamental assumptions are:

- That the world is benevolent

- That the world is meaningful

- That the self is worthy

If we relate these to theories of attachment (e.g. Bowlby, 1980 and Fahlberg, 1991) we can see that the dependent child needs to develop at a very early stage some primal version of these theories of the world if they are to make adequate contact with their environment to enable them to survive infancy.

In their total dependence the infant needs to believe that if they perform certain attachment behaviours the environment will respond by providing care; that creates a predisposition to consider that the world is a benevolent place which will nurture us. The infant then needs to believe that the environment will provide adequate and appropriate feedback for them to modify and adapt their behaviour so as to create optimum bonding in the caregiver; here is a predisposition to search for meaning and structure. This combination of the benevolent environment and the meaningful response of that environment to the attachment behaviour of the infant then produce the sense of the unfolding and individuating self as worthy, which in turn generates new and increasingly effective social interaction. The child thus securely attached to a well-bonded caregiver is the child most likely to survive the total dependency of infancy.

The primacy of these highly abstract schemas as the survival toolkit of the otherwise helpless infant indicates the source of the amazing persistence of the core assumptions we have about the world. Most adults, according to Janoff-Bulman (1992, pp 6-12), believe that they live in a benevolent, safe world rather than a malevolent hostile one; they continue to believe this even if the world appears to be treating them very badly, sometimes adducing very convoluted reasons why it makes sense for them to see themselves as 'lucky' or 'better off than others' to allow for the existence of a benevolent space which is their world even if the world beyond is manifestly destructive. Proverbs again provide clues to this order of thinking: 'there's always someone worse off than you are' we are told, or 'count your blessings'.

People also, she claims, persist in ascribing meaningfulness to the world however powerful the evidence to the contrary may seem. Without a sense of meaning there is no control, no justice, no sense of personal efficacy; without meaning, people are helpless in the face of an impersonal and irrational cosmos. Confronted with loss of control or massive injustice, people may devise complex cosmologies or universal moral systems which explain the essential underlying meaning or justice of the events. 'God moves in a mysterious way' the hymn writer tells us, or 'man proposes, God disposes' proverbially explains our inability to manage or understand events which are part of a greater cosmic plan.

Finally, people continue to believe that they are worthy, that they are in some sense good and valuable human beings who can have an effect on others through relating to them positively. Again this remains true long past the point when we might imagine it would have been abandoned. Convicted prisoners will characteristically justify themselves by comparison with other criminals of lower status, often the hated 'nonces' or child molesters. And those convicted of child molestation may justify themselves against some more heinous version, as they see it, of crimes against children.

These core assumptions may be held by people who appear to be denying them. Where disconfirming evidence is strong, the first line of defence is often to fall back on a modified form of the basic constructs. A realistic negative assessment may be tempered with an exception clause, so that the world may be a terrible place, but at least my home is cosy, or a negative life experience may have cosmic significance ascribed to it, so that suffering in this vale of tears will turn out to be redemptive in the next life, and so on.

It can be seen that at some level our most fundamental assumptions are illusions. Yet without them our capacity to function is seriously diminished. We are creatures who need a measure of optimism, a regular strong dose of unreality, to live life to the full. We need accuracy so far as possible in our superficial schemas, so these, whilst persistent, are generally less well defended and more open to adaptation, which we call learning. But we need our core schemas to be stable and persistent despite the fact that the lives of most of us would offer considerable disconfirming evidence. These most basic assumptions are therefore well defended and highly resistant to change. In the normal run of things we simply fail to notice evidence which disconfirms our core assumptions, or we discredit such evidence without putting it to the test of rational thought. To draw again on the power of proverbs, we decide that it constitutes 'the exception that proves the rule'.

We can now see the force of Janoff-Bulman's argument. Our core assumptions are absolutely necessary to our well-being, yet they have a built-in fragility, for they are constructs which do not accurately represent the world as it is. At the very centre of the human mind is our capacity to represent the world as other than it is, that is, our ability to make symbolic representations, to create language.

Language is the main instrument of man's refusal to accept the world as it is. Without that refusal, without the unceasing generation by the mind of 'counter-worlds' — a generation which cannot be divorced from the grammar of counter-factual and optative forms — we would turn forever on the treadmill of the present. ... Ours is the ability, the need, to gainsay or 'un-say' the world, to image and speak it otherwise (Steiner, 1992 (1975), p228; emphasis in the original).

Our defences against the shattering of our core assumptions are very strong but may not withstand the onslaught of traumatic stress. Events which can at a single stroke expose and demolish the illusions which sustain us, and rob us of the centres of language, symbol and metaphor which would allow us to rebuild a viable and sustainable construct are truly dangerous events. These are wounds to the human mind and human spirit beside which mere physical injuries pale into insignificance.

Luis was called in to see the man who said he shot his (Luis') wife. ... They put him in a closet where he could only stand or sit. He was there for ten days. He survived by separating his body from his brain. The worst point came after several days, when insects entered the box. His hands and fingers were badly infected as were his testicles, and insects were crawling over him. 'I thought I was going to go mad. That's the great fear. Greater than death. Going mad.' His brain devised avenues of escape. He would imagine, for instance, that he was playing the piano (The Pinochet regime in Chile, *The Independent*, 20 October 1998).

Victims of extreme torture often speak afterwards of the fear of going mad as being greater than the fear of death or physical pain. The destruction of their most basic understanding of the world seems more terrifying than the destruction of their bodies or, indeed, of life itself. It is not unreasonable, even in the most extreme situations imaginable, to construe the intense destructiveness of traumatic stress as having to do with the destruction of our core assumptions, our fundamental understanding of the world in which we live.

This understanding of trauma as the destruction of fundamental assumptions fits well with the experience of victims of post traumatic stress disorder. The central concerns of victims beyond immediate safety and management of physiological symptoms are the creation, or re-creation, of a sense of meaning and purpose in life, the rebuilding of trust, and the re-establishment of satisfying personal and social relationships. These concerns seem to match the concept of trauma having destroyed the core constructs of meaning and value in the life of the victim.

The interpretation of trauma as the shattering of assumptions also gives us a route into understanding how people who have not themselves been victims of trauma may become secondary or tertiary victims.

Vulnerability and resilience

If a car carrying passengers crashes, each of the people involved will be affected differently. The causes of these differences will be complex to unravel, but if the situation requires it experts in the field can reconstruct with some accuracy the course of the accident and, in collaboration with medical staff, come to an understanding of the injuries of each of the victims.

Many of the factors involved will be situational: How fast was the car travelling? What did it hit? Where on the car was the point of impact? What sort of car was it? What were the weather and road conditions at the time? Where in the car was the victim sitting? Some will be behavioural, with the injuries relating to the behaviour of individual victims: Were they wearing seat-belts? Had they been using intoxicants? Were they awake or asleep? How did they behave immediately after the crash? And some will be dependent on the individual vulnerability and resilience of each victim: How old are they? How healthy arc they? Do they have a history of previous injuries?

Trauma is an injury, and is equally variable in its impact on victims. As with physical injuries, across a population affected by an injurious event the more destructive the event, the less influence individual vulnerabilities will have on the outcome for that population. For each individual victim, of course, the process of recovery will be dependent on their own unique pattern of strengths and weaknesses, their vulnerability and their resilience.

The historical, political, social and personal denial of the reality of trauma in our society has led to a situation in which there remains a strong tendency to blame the victim. Those who suffer from post traumatic stress disorder are still likely to find themselves regarded as personally weak or behaviourally reprehensible for becoming victims when others survive apparently unscathed. This is a reversal of social attitudes to physical injuries after accidents or disasters, when victims are generally treated with concern and sympathy and those who survive without injury are seen as 'lucky'.

As a result of research and publicity, the tendency to blame the victim of post traumatic stress disorder after specific catastrophic events seems to be diminishing. Victims of occupational traumatic stress are still a long way from general recognition of the nature and effect of their injuries, however, even in occupations which are known to be highly toxic. The process by which we learn, as a community, the costs and implications of the burdens we lay upon individuals willing to undertake necessary but dangerous tasks is work in progress.

Workers in the field of paedophilia have not yet reached the starting point in this debate. My observations suggest that the casualty rates are high, yet I have seen no indication of a formal acknowledgement of the toxicity of the work, and the nature of the injuries which may be sustained by workers, in any of the agencies employing the people who have talked to me, let alone achieving such recognition in the wider community.

The consequence of this lack of recognition of toxicity is that victims of post traumatic stress disorder can find themselves being further victimised by the attitudes of others. Their suffering is likely to be seen as the result of their personal vulnerability to stress, rather than their vulnerability being seen as one of the factors influencing their recovery from injury.

The ground of the debate must be shifted, so that we begin with an understanding that each one of us through the unique and awesome complexity of our individual development has generated intricate patterns of vulnerability and resilience. There can be no clarity of definition here. Strengths and weaknesses are often entirely dependent on context; an attribute may be a strength in one situation and an area of vulnerability in another. Even within the same situation, an attribute may be a strength in terms of one aspect of the task and a weakness in terms of another. Empathy may be a strength in working with children, may even be a requirement of the job, yet may be a source of vulnerability when confronted with the somatised wordless horror of the victim of post traumatic stress disorder after sexual abuse. Dissociation as the capacity to split into different selves in order to get through difficult and dangerous work may be a necessity for working on certain high risk tasks, yet may be an indicator of vulnerability to the development of post traumatic stress disorder.

Many of the attributes which make people suitable for employment in the professions which become involved in dealing with the effects of paedophilia are qualities, tendencies, or attitudes which will produce either increased vulnerability or increased resilience under the impact of traumatic stress. It can also happen that the factor which leads to vulnerability at one stage of recovery from trauma will be exactly the same factor enhancing resilience at a later stage of the process. A vivid visual imagination, for example, may contribute both to injury, generating haunting images of torture and abuse, and to recovery, contributing to the process of learning to manage physiological responses.

The field of traumatic stress is so complex, and so relatively underdeveloped in the history of psychological and psychiatric research, that there are no clear answers on factors which increase vulnerability or enhance resilience. It may be that the chaotic nature of the human response to traumatic stress, the interchangeability of weaknesses and strengths, the dynamic unpredictability of the disorder and of the processes of recovery, mean that there never will be any clear answers. It is nevertheless possible to indicate factors which seem to contribute to vulnerability and resilience.

Factors increasing vulnerability

Drawing out from experience and study (e.g. McFarlane and Yehuda in van der Kolk et al, 1996, p157) some factors which seem most influential in contributing to the likelihood that people will suffer disorder as a result of traumatic stress, it is possible to relate these briefly to the experiences of workers in the field of organised child sexual abuse.

Previous unresolved trauma

People who have previously been victims of trauma have an increased vulnerability to traumatic stress, particularly if the prior trauma was accommodated but not resolved. A survey undertaken by the journal Community Care (June 1995) indicated that one in three of the child care social workers responding to the survey 'admitted' to having suffered some sort of abuse in childhood. This is interesting both in terms of the high proportion of respondents who had been traumatised as children, and in terms of the language used to describe their attitude to their history in relation to their employment. Partial as this survey result is, it might indicate that significant numbers of social workers may be gaining their energy and motivation in an often thankless task from the traumatic experiences of their own childhood.

They will not be the only profession where this is true. It is common for those who survive trauma to dedicate themselves to working for others who are suffering. This is true whether or not they recall the childhood trauma fully, or suffer traumatic amnesia in relation to it. It seems that traumatic stress which does not give rise to post traumatic stress disorder can generate energy and motivation, but it will also leave a lasting vulnerability.

> I wish to acknowledge the frighteningly large role that personal agendas and chance played in this dreadful story. Would those who fought for three years to expose the truth have carried on, if we had not on some level identified with the children in Islington's indifferent care?
>
> The key whistleblower had suffered heartbreaking personal tragedies, which left them fearlessly protective of other children. I myself left an unhappy home at sixteen years of age for bed-sits. ... Genuine concern ... kept our unusually close team digging (Eileen Fairweather, journalist, in Hunt, 1998, p39).

Lack of social support

Those who lack a secure supportive network are more likely to experience post traumatic stress disorder. It is a striking feature of work in the field of paedophilia that previously stable structures of support can collapse leaving the worker unexpectedly exposed and vulnerable. People commonly discovered that professional, organisational, social and personal networks of support all proved inadequate to contain the experiences encountered in this work.

Lack of a safe environment

Workers are often personally threatened when they become involved in investigating paedophile activities or caring for the victims.

Threatening telephone calls are common, often to workers' homes, often late at night; such calls include death threats, silent calls, and threats to harm family members. Foster carers have needed to change shopping habits and children have needed to change schools. Whilst an element of threat may be expected in public service work, I have not found so great an intensity and variety of threats across such a range of disciplines in any other area of work.

Subsequent trauma

Workers are likely to experience not one single traumatic event but rather a series of experiences that build up a traumatic stress response. The result might more properly be called prolonged duress stress disorder (Kinchin, 1998, p8) than post traumatic stress disorder, but the symptoms are said to be the same, and where staff have been assessed and diagnosed as symptomatic it has been a diagnosis of post traumatic stress disorder which has been applied.

In the case of organised and network child sexual abuse, all the victims, the children who are primary victims, families who may be secondary victims and workers who may be tertiary victims, suffer repeated traumatisation rather than one disastrous event. The implications of this seem to be an increased likelihood of developing post traumatic stress disorder.

Poor communication skills

Most, though not all, people who work in this field will have been selected for the work because they have good communication skills, so it may be thought that this vulnerability factor will not be relevant. However a common theme in the stories I have heard was the experience of being silenced. Paedophilia generates circles of harm and domains of silence. The experience can be devastating for professionals who have spent their working life honing skills in communicating the truth clearly and openly. For many people, across a range of professional disciplines, the blocking of communication can be one of the most harmful experiences in this whole toxic field of work.

Here are the words of two workers from quite different disciplines, written as journal entries at the time of their involvement in working with victims of organised abuse:

I shout
They do not hear

I shout and shout
They can not hear

Professional abuse
By managers
Who cannot hear
Me shout

Who will not hear
Me shout

The shouting will
Get louder
And stronger

Because children
Cannot
And do not
Shout

I've been brave ever since
But I'm sick of it.
I'm sick of being terrified by what I've learned
And literally sick from not being able to tell it.

I've the constitution of an ox, me,
But even I can't cope with tough ex-coppers
Near to tears
And too frightened to go on the record.
Remember my endless tonsillitis?
My throat swollen by all the secrets I cannot say.

You think I'm mad
I think I'm silenced
All I know is children are getting hurt out there
And none of us are stopping it

Reactions at the time of the trauma

Victims who believe that they responded 'well' or 'appropriately' at the time of trauma seem to be less likely to develop post traumatic stress disorder (McFarlane and Yehuda in van der Kolk *et al*, 1996, p156). Many of those who have spoken to me believe that they did the best they could in the circumstances, but are nevertheless haunted by a sense that they have in some way failed the children.

The repetitive nature of the traumatic stress, arriving from all sorts of directions, allows for a host of different reactions at the time of each separate traumatic experience, so that few escape without a nagging sense of something for which they may reproach themselves. People who felt they did well in interview with the child may feel that they did badly in court, people who felt they did well with managing day to day disordered behaviour from the child may feel they did badly in eliciting support and resources from their management, people who felt they did well in first noticing the signs of abuse may feel they did badly when confronted with the press, and so on.

Prior personality traits

There are some indications that people who have a tendency to neuroticism are more vulnerable to post traumatic stress disorder. It is impossible for me to comment on the personality profiles of victims before the experience of traumatic stress. Nearly all studies of post traumatic stress disorder are retrospective; this is not surprising, since it is, in most circumstances, part of the nature of trauma that it strikes unexpectedly. The people who have talked to me have done so because they had been involved in work related to paedophilia, so if they had been traumatised by the work it had already happened by the time I heard their story.

All that can reasonably be said is to reiterate that the people in any organisation who become involved in this area of work are likely to be those who have a history of stability and a good record of employment. If they had a tendency to neuroticism it probably was not causing them any problems beforehand.

Past or family history of mental illness

There is some evidence that a personal or family history of mental illness is a predictor for an enhanced risk of post traumatic stress disorder after exposure to traumatic stress. This may be something for people to bear in mind when preparing themselves, or helping colleagues prepare for, taking part in work which is known to be toxic; it may also be important information for managing self and others through the course of such work.

In considering the process of developing post traumatic stress disorder McFarlane and Yehuda (van der Kolk et al, 1996, p157) note that:

> The individual's response at each step of this process will be influenced by a complex matrix of biological, social, temperamental, and experiential issues. ... Some characteristics increase the probability of a pathological outcome. These are 'vulnerability' factors; they are generally neither necessary nor sufficient to explain the onset of a disorder or predict its course, but rather place the individual at risk of a negative outcome.

Factors increasing resilience

There are also factors which make us strong. This strength, the strength to weather trauma without being destroyed, though we may be transformed, is the strength of saplings in the wind. It is not brittle. It is resilience, not resistance.

Previous resolved trauma

Traumatic stress leaves indelible scars. If the trauma has been worked through and integrated into our lives, the scars can become a map to guide us through subsequent traumatic events and situations. Although people who have suffered previous trauma have an added vulnerability, a sensitivity to destructive threat, they also have reserves of experience, knowledge and insight to enable them to find or create the resources to survive.

Secure social support

The best protector against being destroyed by traumatic stress is social support, secure attachment relationships within the context of a network of reliable social relationships. The individual whose social support network can sustain the onslaught of the destructive traumatic stress and continue to hold the person safe as they wrestle with the shattering of assumptions and the collapse of meaning is far more likely to come through to the other side.

A safe environment

People who can find or retain a safe space, a place which is not just objectively secure but which actually feels secure, have an area to which they can retreat and a healing space within which they can recuperate.

Good communication skills

On the journey through the war zone of traumatic stress it is essential to keep open the lines of communication. Being able to translate the experience into a language, to make meaningful symbols which mark out the path we have taken through the maze, allows us in due course to integrate the trauma into the story of our life without being destroyed by it. When the traumatic stress includes silencing, and being deprived of a voice is part of the horror, then those who can find a means of expression are increasing their resilience. Turning to some non-verbal means of self-expression may reopen the doors of communication; people may find release through dance, music, or, as in the case of Frida Kahlo who became a great artist, through putting paint on canvas, expressing the pain in vivid pictures.

> I paint everything: my lips, my blood-red fingernails, eyelids, my earlobes, my eyelashes, my eyebrows. ... I paint myself over and over again. Two of me exist, and as I paint I exorcise the wounded, second Frida (Frida Kahlo, painter, quoted in *Frida Kahlo: The Camera Seduced*, Chronicle Books, 1992).

Prior personality traits

Just as neuroticism may be a predictor for increased vulnerability, so stability and adaptability as enduring personality traits are protectors against being destroyed by traumatic stress. Fortunately many of those who find themselves beset by traumatic stress as a result of working in the area of organised child sexual abuse are likely to be stable and adaptable people, for those who move into child protection work or caring for traumatised children have often been selected on the basis of criteria which identify stability and adaptability as necessary qualities.

Religious faith

Many systems of religious belief are 'virtually immune to empirical disconfirmation' (Tedeschi and Calhoun, 1995, p116), and can contribute to resilience by sustaining a sense of meaning and purpose far beyond the limits of individual cognitive constructs. On the other hand, people who have had a religious faith and who find that it disintegrates as their meaning world collapses are bereft indeed. The balance seems to be that religious faith contributes more to resilience than to vulnerability.

Religious faith in this context should be taken in the broadest sense of a system of transcendent beliefs carrying meaning for the believer, or an organised cultural system of beliefs, or a sense of cosmic trust which may be linked to religious rituals or practices. The interaction with traumatic stress is complex. Faith may provide a sense of meaning or transcendent structure, or a community of support, or a set of practices which may provide meaningful activity and a sense of effectiveness in the face of meaningless horror.

Faith is the strength by which a shattered world shall emerge into the light. Helen Keller.

Insight

The remaining six 'resiliencies', beginning with insight, are drawn from *The Resilient Self* (Wolin and Wolin, 1993). People who know about trauma and the effect of traumatic stress are less vulnerable and more resilient (see Ursano, Grieger and McCarroll in van der Kolk *et al*, 1996, p448). If they are also aware of inner processes, and able to relate the knowledge to the experience, then their capacity to withstand the destructiveness of traumatic stress is greatly enhanced.

Autonomy

We need social support to survive trauma, but we also need to be able to stand alone, to be aware of an internal locus of control which is accessible even when events are catastrophically out of control. At the worst times the autonomous self may be present only as the inner observer, the self who notices in the midst of chaos how interesting it all is.

Initiative

People who can remain or become assertive and active when experiencing traumatic stress are more likely to emerge unharmed though they cannot emerge unchanged.

Creativity

Traumatic stress, the catastrophic deconstruction of our structures of meaning, will be encountered with greater resilience by those who know how to play. The origin of all creativity, a playful nature allows us to image worlds which do not exist, to generate new structures out of the ruins of the old, or to conjure fresh landscapes of order and meaning out of the thin air of chaos.

Humour

Close kin to creativity, humour is the shifting of perspectives which may discover and illuminate the space on which, in a shifting landscape, it is safe to stand. As Douglas Adams reminds us in *The Restaurant at the End of the Universe*, if we could see the whole universe the perspective would destroy us, and the 'Total Perspective Vortex' is the ultimate punishment. Traumatic stress can feel like that. The sudden shift in our inner world, dropping us off into the abyss, depositing us in the void, can leave us with a dizzying loss of perspective.

People who characteristically appreciate the humour of their own situation, who have a grasp of the ironies of life and the capacity to view things from more than one perspective, are more resilient to trauma.

Morality

Those who have a strong sense of a moral order are significantly more resilient than those lacking such schemas. People who believe that there are values which inform and give meaning to our actions have access to an energy which Robert Coles in his study of highly resilient children called 'moral energy' (Coles, 1986).

'Moral energy is a life-sustaining force that can lift survivors above the downward tug of hardship' (Wolin and Wolin, 1993, p188). For people who work in the highly toxic field of paedophile abuse, the sense of devotion to service and of being willing to make sacrifices for a greater cause than personal comfort or happiness, the sense of a supervening moral order is likely to be both a motivator and a sustainer in carrying the work through to completion. It is the energy which will keep us going when the world is collapsing around us, the strong centre which will hold us firm and keep us telling our truth.

> ... we can tell you what we know. The past is a hard stone within us. On this subject we have become unmoveable, implacable. There is no way of convincing us otherwise, we say, ... we know what we know (*Woman and Nature: the roaring inside her,* Susan Griffin, 1984, p216).

Chapter 7

Tertiary victimisation
casualties of work

O the mind, mind has mountains; cliffs of fall
Frightful, sheer, no-man-fathomed. Hold them cheap
May who ne'er hung there. Nor does long our small
Durance deal with that steep or deep. Here! creep,
Wretch, under a comfort serves in a whirlwind: all
Life death does end and each day dies with sleep.
– 'No worst', Gerard Manley Hopkins

What happens to them, these professional people, these police officers and teachers, social workers and foster carers, lawyers and doctors, nurses and therapists? These are experienced workers in highly stressful jobs, tough and resourceful people, used to being immersed in the seamier side of life, case hardened, even. What happens to them that they can be found at three in the morning driving out into the country to find a quiet place to sit in their cars and scream? What makes them shiver so when the sun is shining, and lay their heads on the desks and weep when the last of their colleagues has left the office?

The description which follows of the experiences and symptoms which arise from work in the field of paedophilia was drawn from conversations with several hundred people over seven years. It fits well with work in the United States on vicarious or secondary traumatisation, such as *Secondary Traumatic Stress* (B. Hudnall Stamm, 1995), although there are additional specific issues which arise in dealing with paedophilia. This descriptive list was then discussed thoroughly with thirty people from diverse settings in various parts of the country who had significant involvement in work around paedophilia. More than 90% said that they and their colleagues between them, another hundred or so workers in the field, had suffered all of the listed experiences and symptoms. The indefinite quantifiers 'some', 'many', 'most' and so on were drawn from my initial conversations and reinforced by the observations of these thirty people. This process was not intended to emulate or replace rigorous research on the subject, but rather to prompt such research and suggest directions for it.

It begins, let us say, with the children. It may not it may begin with the seizure of pornographic materials, or an inspection of a residential establishment, or a manager reviewing case material who realises that records simply do not fit together. But often it begins with the children. A chance remark to a teacher or carer, a homework exercise 'What I did last week' that just for once gets behind the child's defences, the death of a pet, some little thing will happen to light the long fuse of discovery.

These are often children who have been telling us for a long time through their behaviour that all is not well with their world. The chaos which is the trademark of trauma will have been spilling out into so many areas of life. If they have avoided the facile labels: 'disruptive', 'manipulative', 'aggressive', 'learning disability', 'offending behaviour', and all the other tags which may protect us from noticing the pain, then people may already have been asking questions about the roots of the disordered behaviour.

In any case, at some point someone has to be open to notice the throwaway comment, the hand the child offers us so very tentatively and so briefly to see if we will grasp it and hold them safe. As I study the history of these investigations, I am left wondering how many of these hands raised above the waters in which children are drowning are being ignored day by day.

It is not that we are consciously callous, only that it is always hard to see the signals of distress which we unconsciously recognise may disrupt our lives. An early memory: my best friend's father drowned while trying to rescue someone swept out to sea, who later was swept onto shore and survived. Half a lifetime later, at the Elephant and Castle, home of the then Department of Health and Social Security, I attend a discussion on child prostitution – 'What child prostitution?' ask the men in grey suits, and yet I know they must have stepped across the same young bodies I had needed to navigate to reach the building.

For the process of discovery to begin, someone has to notice what is happening to the children. Or rather, someone has to notice that something very powerful and destructive is happening to the children. There are procedures for the protection of children, and we live in a society committed to promoting the safety and welfare of children; in theory it should be possible to set out the process which will follow that first raising of concern. In practice, of course, things are always different from the theory. The course of any investigation will be fraught with difficulties. There will be problems with resources, problems with staffing, problems with liaison between agencies, and, if it ever gets that far, the inevitable problems with criminal proceedings in cases involving child sexual abuse.

Those are the run of the mill problems, the difficulties which every experienced worker in any of the agencies involved will know with frustrating and frustrated familiarity. Paedophilia cases develop differently, however. Something happens in cases involving organised or network child sexual abuse that makes the experience different. It does not always happen in the same way; every case has its own watershed, its own point of no return for the health and well-being of the workers. Beyond that point the case starts to chew people up, and outside observers begin to notice casualties. There seem to be four things in particular which such cases have in common, producing the high toxicity of work in the field of organised and network child sexual abuse.

The conspiracy

There is no getting away from the fact that organised child sexual abuse is a conspiracy, in the exact sense of the word: *a combination of persons for an evil or unlawful purpose; an agreement between two or more to do something criminal, illegal, or reprehensible* (OED). Even paedophiles who seem to be operating alone are likely to be linked to others through the internet, through the use of pornography, or through membership of paedophile shared interest groups. Paedophiles conspire together to commit crimes.

At some point when working in this field, workers will be brought up against the reality that paedophile conspiracies involve a lot of people. They will have to face the fact that they do not know who are the paedophiles in their own community. Or worse still, they will have to live with the fact that they do know who are the paedophiles in their own community, or at least some of them. They will be forced to confront the knowledge that respected and valued members of the community are secretly engaged in the sexual abuse of children. No profession is exempt; doctors, nurses, priests, teachers, social workers, police officers, may all be part of local, national, or international paedophile networks. People who do this work have to do so with the knowledge that they cannot be sure which of their colleagues they can trust and which of their superiors may be involved.

The nature of the abuse
Case hardened as these workers may be, the stories they will have to hear as they set out to unravel the complexities of organised or network child sexual abuse are likely to stick in the imagination and in the memory. All of us have heard things we can never forget, however hard we may try. Police officers have to sit through hours of pornographic videos in order to amass evidence of identity, of the offenders and of their victims. Carers may live with children who re-enact elements of the abuse obsessively, harming themselves terribly over and over again as they try to integrate the horror by replaying it. Therapists, if they are available and anyone is prepared to pay for them, provide a safe space for the victims to explore what has happened; one therapist said: 'This work contaminates. It's like a poison, it gets under your skin and spreads to infect everything you do.'

The experience of being silenced
When these elements are mixed together what is produced is potent and poisonous. Professionals working with this material at some point commonly find themselves confronted with the experience of being silenced. They are used to confidentiality, they know how to hold their tongues, but they expect to be able to speak and write and negotiate and use language appropriately to the service for which they are employed.

It may be when a case starts to look exceedingly complicated and complex, and many of them are, for that is the nature of conspiracies. Take your little child abuse investigation, get on with it quietly, and all may yet be well. Discover that this case has links to networks in other places, and see how quickly the shutters fall. By their nature these are multi-agency investigations, struggling to manage the complexities of liaison and funding and working to different agendas.

Once the door is opened to the possibility that there may be much wider implications, the sheer logistics of it all becomes a nightmare. At this point workers may feel that what they have to say is no longer being heard, that the evidence they have gathered is going nowhere; the experience is one of being silenced. The effect is both deskilling and disempowering. Here are children and wounded adults tearing their hearts out to try to tell us what has happened to them. Here we are entrusted with the task of making use of the information they are giving us, at such personal cost, to make the community safer for children. That is, after all, what we are employed to do. And now we are proving completely ineffective in getting the message across.

The same experience, but from a very different source, may occur at the point where the names being raised belong to people who are perceived to be influential or powerful. Again, it is irrelevant whether this is actually the cause of the closing down of communication. Once the workers in the case feel that they are no longer being heard, the perception that this is linked to the power or influence of the perpetrators is enough to render the experience highly toxic.

The experience of being threatened

It is a measure of the toxicity of this work that so many people who have spoken to me have separately and independently come to the same areas of perceived experience, expressed in very similar forms of words. It is very common for people to feel that they have been robbed of a voice, that they have been deprived of the capacity to speak their truth. This is language very reminiscent of the way primary victims speak of being silenced.

Being threatened is, for workers in this field, a matter both of objective fact and of individual and shared perception. There are actual threats, including telephone death threats, repeated silent calls in the early hours of the morning, telephone calls relating to the movements or activities of family members, especially the worker's children or grandchildren, and so on. There are experiences which may be intended to be threats, such as vandalism to property. And then there is a general shared sense of dangerousness which seems to be widespread and pervasive. There is a collective undertow of fear which is very striking.

Traumatic stress
No matter how tough and experienced, everyone has their own set of core assumptions which are the most basic theories through which they construe the world and make sense of their environment. That just seems to be the way our brains work. If people are managing to sustain a life in public service, then there must be enough of a positive bias in their core assumptions about the world to create the energy and motivation to keep going in such demanding work.

Working with the effects of paedophilia seems to get in among those fundamental assumptions and shatter them. When that happens the result is traumatic stress. Not stress, which this group of workers have probably lived with for years and are practised in managing, but traumatic stress, which knocks out, at the same time, the most central metaphors by which we understand the world and the creative centres of language and symbolic imagery which would allow us to repair the damage.

Many people find that the onslaught of traumatic stress has an impact on their daily lives. They begin to notice that they are being injured. Others, more psychologically defended against the noticing, though not against the injury, will deny being affected, but bear the marks in their lives. Some cease to be able to function adequately, and remove themselves from the danger, or find themselves removed by sickness. Almost everyone I have heard from or spoken to on the subject notices a qualitative difference between this area of work and other, perhaps outwardly similar, work they have undertaken.

The crucial difference for many people is the pervasive nature of the effects of this work. It seems that the traumatic stress which may arise through becoming involved in work in the field of paedophilia can produce effects which have an impact on the personal, social and professional life of the victim.

Personal health

It is common for people working in this field to report disruption to their usual pattern of physical health or mental health or both. For some this disruption has been troublesome but more or less temporary. Others experience some degree of permanent change in their health. Symptoms reported include:

Sleep disturbance

There may be difficulty falling asleep, or early waking, or both. For some people this has begun with, or been exacerbated by, night time telephone calls which have proved impossible to trace but which may take the form of overt threats or silent wake up calls in the small hours of the morning. Received over a period of time at irregular intervals, these can be very disruptive of sleep patterns. Some people have needed medication to help them sleep, including people who have never previously used such medication.

Some people have experienced nightmares or night terrors. The content of nightmares, where that is meaningful, may seem to be related to received threats or be related to the subject matter of the children's revelations. Night terrors, in which people wake suddenly in a state of terror without any awareness of an accompanying dream, are particularly common.

Workers in the field sometimes report having needed much more sleep than usual but still feeling constantly tired. They may feel so drained that life contracts to become almost nothing more than work and sleep.

Appetite disturbance

It is striking how often people have spoken of not being able to eat or not being able to stop eating. Having spent so many years caring for children who had suffered traumatic stress, I had noticed the disruptions in appetite which seem to be common. Now here were adult workers expressing the same patterns of symptoms after victimisation.

Speaking of the experience of traumatic stress, many people will point to the region of their solar plexus. What they describe is the feeling of a hard lump, like stone, or a hard knot which sometimes loosens a little giving rise to sensations of cold and trembling. It is noticeable that this is a widespread experience, echoed in much of the language of poetry and descriptive prose, like the line from Susan Griffin, 'The past is a hard stone within us.'

Here we have people who are adept in the use of language and who may also be professionally adept in recognising and expressing feelings, for whom it is clear that a feeling has become somatised. When describing this people do not say 'I feel anxious', or 'I feel terrified', which would be congruent both with the sensation and with other non-verbal signs as they describe what is happening. What they say is 'I feel a hard lump here in my middle' . They may add adjectives such as fluttering, shaky, or cold, to describe the lump or knot more fully.

The disrupted eating patterns are often related to this inner sensation, which seems to have a life of its own. People feel that they cannot eat because they will be sick, because the stone or lump will interfere with digestion, or because there is simply no space inside them for food. Or they stuff themselves with food because this alters the sensation and gives a feeling of having some control over it.

When they do eat, digestive problems are common. Indigestion, heartburn, flatulence and diarrhoea are all frequently reported, and often related by the victim to the presence of this sensation of a lump or knot. This somatised response in tertiary victims is striking. It is almost a trademark for workers in this field: ask them how they feel about the work and at some point they are likely to make this telltale gesture towards the solar plexus, whilst being curiously unable to produce congruent words for their emotions. Trauma may start in our heads, but it lives in our middles.

Decreased resistance to infection

Staff in this area of work have a very high commitment to keeping going at all costs, and a high rate of sickness. This suggests that workers are feeling quite ill a fair amount of the time, which indeed is how people say they feel. Taken as a whole population, this is not a sickly bunch of people – they would be unlikely to be selected to do this type of work if they were. Many are bewildered by the range of illnesses with which they are afflicted. Colds, flu, throat infections, chest infections – people whose previous medical record was more or less blank can find themselves taking antibiotics as if they were food supplements.

Increase in stress related conditions

Such conditions as asthma, migraine, headaches, skin eruptions, alopecia, irritable bowel syndrome, and aching joints, may develop for the first time or be exacerbated in the course of this work. Conditions which were previously fully managed may become almost or actually disabling.

Anxiety

Workers may develop generalised anxiety. This is sometimes expressed in words but more often takes the form of obsessive behaviours such as double checking household security, always checking the car for tampering, carrying a personal alarm, and obsessively checking on the security of family members. Most of these are simply exaggerations of behaviours which are entirely reasonable in the light of threats issued. It is the extension into a generalised state of fear or anxiety or obsessive double checking which indicates that sensible precautions are becoming a problem.

On the whole it was astonishing to discover how far people managed not to generalise the anxiety. At no time did I encounter anything un-balanced or out of proportion in the comments made to me. People made determined and successful efforts to maintain a sense of per-spective and rationality, in circumstances when many less balanced would have been tipped over into paranoid fantasies. If anything, it was clear that workers underplayed the impact of the sense of threat and dangerousness inherent in this work.

Despite the calm exterior, panic attacks were not infrequent. Those who suffered them had often just accepted that this was now a feature of their lives. People described dealing calmly with difficult situations, then on the journey home needing to pull off the road to wait for an attack of shaking terror to pass. Sometimes there was a sense of shame or inadequacy in the telling, almost as though the more competently someone had lived their lives for thirty or forty or fifty years, the more they felt ashamed of reactions which they perceived as weakness.

Some people reported the development of phobic symptoms. They found themselves developing a panic state associated with particular places or activities, and had developed a fixed pattern of avoidance wherever possible.

Depression

Most people had experienced depression at some point in being involved in this work. For those with no history of depressive illness this can be a frightening experience in itself. The 'cliffs of fall, frightful, sheer, no-man-fathomed' to which we may find ourselves clinging are very different from any previous experience of feeling a bit miserable. Most of those I spoke to who commented on the depression they suffered were people whose usual temperament was sanguine rather than melancholy. Accustomed to feeling cheerful and optimistic, it was devastating to find themselves facing the bleak emptiness of depression.

Some spoke with passionate intensity of the gradual loss of interest in their environment, the loss of a sense that anything mattered, the feeling that life and joy and colour had drained out of their world, the experience of living life in a deep grey mist that shrouded and muted all sensation and destroyed the quality of life.

Others had never regained the sparkle, but seemed to have settled for a life in monotone. They described themselves as burnt out, or reckoned that they were lucky to have survived and had stopped expecting to feel better. Some had opted for work which they regarded as less demanding but which they also found tedious. Others had moved out of their professional field altogether, and generally expressed a sense of shame that, as they saw it, they had not proved adequate to the task.

Loss of energy

This may be a subset of depression, but it seemed to be experienced as a separate symptom as well. There is a sense of being permanently physically drained of energy, as though suddenly energy has become a rationed commodity and what is on offer for each day just will not match the hours available. People generally describe the depression as having a feeling content, whereas this is an experience which is affect neutral. It is a physical nuisance, like losing the sense of smell when you have a cold in the head.

Sexual dysfunction

Many people developed sexual difficulties whilst involved in this work. Reports include loss of libido, reduction in enjoyment, and loss of sexual function. Some of the problems seemed to be linked to depression, repeated illnesses and loss of energy; others were directly linked to the nature of the work, as people described having times of being revolted by the whole idea of having sex, or of wanting to engage in sexual activity and then being interrupted by flashbacks to images from stories heard or videos watched at work.

For some it was their partner whose sexual behaviour changed, the partner who could not accommodate to the thought of the horrors the other had vicariously had to witness. These were particularly painful stories, as individuals who had struggled all day with images of terror turned for comfort to the person they loved and found themselves treated as contaminated. And partners were not generally blamed for their response, which was recognised as unconscious and unintended. After all, they were not alone in sensing that this work is toxic.

Irritability

This is widely reported, by workers themselves and also as the major comment back from family and friends about their own behaviour during the period of involvement in this work. Irritability in people who are normally placid is extremely wearing for partners and families, and is in some ways more difficult to come to terms with than more obvious indicators of psychological injury. Nightmares, panic attacks, sexual dysfunction and tearfulness may be recognised as seriously abnormal behaviours arising from the nature of the work, but snappy responses to simple questions cause disruption in any household.

Inability to concentrate

Loss of concentration was cited often as a troublesome symptom. Most people felt that they had generally managed to hang on to some level of concentration at work but commonly found that concentration on leisure activities dwindled. This exacerbated the sense of emptiness and depression by robbing people of the enjoyment of the activities which they designated for their own relaxation.

Inability to relax

Even when they did pursue leisure activities, many people found it increasingly hard to relax and unwind. This could extend to all forms of relaxation. Professionals who had long since established satisfactory patterns of relaxation from stressful occupations, found their usual strategies for turning off were useless.

Forgetfulness

Whenever I teach about trauma, I find that there is some point in the session when I am discussing amnesia and I lose the plot. I just momentarily forget whatever it was I was about to say. Writing this had exactly the same effect. Forgetfulness is a strange phenomenon.

There were a number of symptoms which were commonly experienced by the people who told me their stories, but which they did not remember until prompted. Loss of memory was one of them. There was no question, I hasten to add, of false memory syndrome here. I did not suggest to people that they had lost some functions of memory, simply presented them with a list of symptoms others had suffered, and asked if any of it made connections.

When prompted, people picked out forgetfulness as a problem they had experienced. They had previously either ascribed their loss of memory to the process of ageing, even though the memory function often improved again when the piece of work ended, or they had forgotten their forgetfulness. Once they remembered it, they recalled that it had felt like a serious problem at the time, and one which caused them considerable shame and distress. This would seem odd to me, except that I also felt shame and distress when my memory would not function.

Tearfulness

This speaks for itself. People who are involved in this sort of work sometimes burst into tears, or find themselves silently weeping into their beer long before they would normally have reached the tearful stage of inebriation.

Emotional lability

If you are used to being stable and dependable and in reasonable but flexible control of your own emotions, it comes as a shock to become subject to sudden attacks of passionate feeling. It is not so much the emotion as the sense of being out of control which disturbs and distresses people who have a strong sense of who they are and this is not it.

Misuse of alcohol and drugs

Many people found that their use of alcohol and tobacco increased during their time involved in this work, sometimes to the point of it becoming a serious problem for them or for their families. Some people became habituated to the use of prescription drugs they had never previously needed. Occasionally I spoke to someone whose own judgement was that they had suffered no ill-effects from doing this work, but whose colleagues and friends saw them as having developed problems with misuse of alcohol. Some of that was about attribution; they may have been experiencing problems with relationships and problems with feelings as well as problems with alcohol, but they attributed different causes to their various sufferings.

Close relationships

Victims of trauma are not the men and women they once were. The central ground on which they built their lives has shifted beneath them and they have been plunged into chaos. Van der Kolk and McFarlane

(1996) speak of trauma as a 'black hole', an area of such unimaginable density that it exerts a gravitational pull on everything that comes near it; nothing within the black hole can escape the intensity of the gravitational field, not even light. As a result we can never see a black hole. The only way we would know that it existed would be by noticing the effect it was having on bodies around it. An intriguing metaphor.

For workers in the field of paedophilia the effects on relationships can be anything from painful to catastrophic, and those in the closest relationships are those most closely affected.

Partners

When we consider the list of health problems which may be generated by tertiary victimisation, it can hardly be surprising that most partner relationships feel the strain and some disintegrate. And that is only looking at what is happening to one of the partners physically and mentally. Add to that list of possible symptoms the recognition that there are also the thoughts and feelings of the other partner to be taken into account, as well as a range of issues to do with family, friends, and the wider community, and it begins to be clear that these will be relationships under strain.

When people change, stable relationships accommodate to those changes. We do not try to freeze people in time, we do not expect our partner in middle age to be the same person we formed a bond with years before; if it were otherwise, no relationship would last out a year. But the changes induced by traumatic stress are of a different order. The strain placed on the partner can be immense, and some previously stable relationships have collapsed under it.

Where partner relationships do survive the onslaughts of traumatic stress on physical health, emotional stability, sexual function and social behaviour, it sometimes happens that the partner takes on a caretaker role: '...caretaking by spouses ... is both common and stressful, with (partners) showing higher levels of intrusive and avoidant symptoms' (Ursano, Grieger and McCarroll in van der Kolk *et al*, 1996, p455).

Children

As well as being irritable and anxious and generally thoroughly unpleasant to live with, tertiary victims who are parents may become overprotective towards their own children. Overprotective parents do harm to their children – that is one of life's little ironies. The parent may have the best of reasons for becoming so unreasonable, but from the point of view of the child the result is the same.

More heartrending are the children who seem to have lost some of their childhood. It is impossible to avoid children becoming involved in the horror when they have to be told that they should not answer the telephone, should not shop in certain areas, and, in extreme but justified circumstances, that they should carry a personal alarm and have safety points built in to the journey on their way home from school.

Children in fostering families live daily with the behaviour of the primary victim, the fostered child. If their parent then becomes a tertiary (or secondary?) victim as well, these children may find themselves carrying heavier burdens than their shoulders can bear.

The social self

It is common for tertiary victims to discover that their social life has disappeared. There are usually several processes involved in this disintegration of social networks.

Social activities previously valued by the victim may cease to have meaning. People who described themselves as 'party animals' before becoming involved in this work then described movingly how they simply could not make sense of their social world. Like Rita and her mother in the film 'Educating Rita', they look around the pub and think 'there must be a better song than this to sing'.

Often it is simply the activity of the black hole of trauma, the impossibility of thinking sensibly, or thinking at all, about anything else, which destroys social relationships Time and again people spoke of their experience of being in a social gathering, being asked an ordinary social question, and finding that their minds had gone completely blank. 'How are you?' says the old friend, or 'What have you been doing with yourself?' and suddenly there you are with your mouth open and no words coming out.

Sometimes people just do not have the energy to be bothered with keeping up social relationships. Sometimes they have the feeling of being contaminated, an extension of the feeling primary victims often expressed: that they are a source of poison in the world. And sometimes they are actually ostracised; there may be publicity, the press may be involved, local community figures may be involved, and suddenly the invitations stop arriving.

The professional self

My own disciplines of residential child care and social work have been critically damaged by paedophilia. The discovery of the extent and nature of organised child sexual abuse within child care has devastated the profession. The devastation is plain to see but remains largely unspoken and unacknowledged. It is inevitable that paedophiles should focus their careers where possible on settings which allow direct access to vulnerable children, and there will be a concentration of organised child sexual abuse within the professional fields that provide that access. Yet it is also becoming clear that no professional field is immune.

All of us are having to learn to work in an altered world where we live with the awareness that some of our colleagues are paedophiles. The process of initiation into this knowledge is part of the process of shattering the assumptions on which the foundations of our professional lives are built. It can destroy us. I have watched people in several professional fields struggle with the recognition that they have worked for half a lifetime with, have respected and trusted, have been students and almost disciples of, colleagues who behind closed doors through all that time have been buggering and raping children, and having it all recorded on video for their friends.

These are circumstances in which it can be very difficult to sustain colleague relationships. The professional self tends to suffer. Those are the kind of understatements I have become accustomed to hearing from the commendably balanced and rational people I have listened to. And words become devalued. When I use the word devastated I do mean laid waste, reduced to rubble and burned out ruins – the shattering of fundamental assumptions.

This is the context in which people must try to conduct intricate investigations into child sexual abuse and look after the children who are the primary victims of the abuse. It is no surprise to discover that difficulties arise. When workers commented on the impact of tertiary victimisation on the professional self, they seemed to perceive four factors as particulary relevant.

The personal impact of traumatic stress on their ability to function as competent professionals is almost universally a matter of concern among these workers. Occasionally this is expressed through avoidance and denial: 'I can't let it get to me or I couldn't carry on with the work'; which is a way of surviving which tends to take its toll in the long run through deteriorating health and relationships. More often workers expressed their concerns that this work presented them with profound challenges in sustaining the standards of professional work they expected of themselves. They were open about this, and tried to address it themselves to the best of their ability, but they often felt that their attempts were largely unsupported at an organisational level and were ineffective.

This perceived lack of support commonly extended to relationships with colleagues at an individual level. Many report being treated with suspicion or actively shunned by previously friendly colleagues. Some have been labelled by colleagues or managers with such epithets as 'hysterical' or 'obsessive' despite the fact that they were dealing with acknowledged and proven cases, and were quite rationally and peaceably setting out the truth as they could see it.

At an organisational level many people I have listened to speak of experiences ranging from lack of appropriate support at the positive end of the scale, to blocking and undermining and sometimes downright bullying and intimidation at the other. Many people reported feeling that the organisation was reflecting the sense of contamination which goes with this work, and that they were regarded with suspicion and distrust after their involvement in it even when they had previously enjoyed high status and esteem within the organisation. There is an overwhelming sense that even the most enlightened of organisations is a long way from being able to manage this sort of work appropriately.

It is not uncommon for workers to report having found themselves involved with the media as a result of their work in this field. There was a sense that this involvement might also have a negative effect professionally, as might contact which may have occurred with various independent 'watchdog' organisations. Sometimes people felt so strongly about this that it had become disabling. On the one hand reports in the media may be very partial and misrepresent the actions of workers in a way which undermines their professional confidence, and on the other hand workers who are whistleblowers may suffer professionally as a result of their decision to take unilateral action.

The political self

Paedophilia is in various ways enmeshed in the social fabric of this country. Paedophiles conspire together to commit crimes, and they continue to do so with relative impunity; this is not conspiracy theory, but a simple statement about the nature of organised child sexual abuse.

> We are often naïve about the degree of contact between abusers. We come across connections between abusers for which we have no explanation. Paedophiles work for each other 24 hours a day, seven days a week. ... I do not, in general, subscribe to the conspiracy theory of events in society, because it requires application and a degree of security that is not normally found. However there is no doubt that paedophiles use a degree of organisation and security that we do not often come across, and we will never deal with them successfully unless we use a strategic approach (Bibby, 1996, p261).

Everyone whose work brings them into contact with organised child sexual abuse will at some point make these discoveries. The experience usually changes them forever.

We can never again place unquestioning trust in any of our social institutions. Not just institutional child care, but the law, the church, the health service, education – all have been tainted. Perhaps this seems abstract, perhaps an accomplished cynic might say that they never did have any unquestioning faith in the society which sustains us all. But it is much more personal and destructive than that. It eats away at the heart of us, this knowledge.

For we do place our trust in social institutions, because we must. We live here. We send our children to playgroup and to school. We encourage them to take part in sports and leisure activities. We send them on trips and outings. We make sure they have access to hospitals, and we send them there when they need it. We make the political decisions necessary to ensure that the most needy children in our community can be cared for. We do all that, and we hope that the children will not be abused.

Most of them will not be abused. The statistics are on our side. But some of them will be. And some of that abuse will happen because we have not understood as a society that paedophilia is part of our social order. Paedophiles are not somewhere else, they are here. Ordinary people living ordinary public lives and extraordinary secret lives, which they can do because like all other ordinary people they have minds which can believe that whatever they most deeply want to do is all right.

The study of trauma teaches us that in response to any stimulus, we first react, then we explain our action to ourselves. Or as Shotter wrote in 1984, 'Instead of thinking before they act, people must in general act before they think, in order later to think before they act' (p46). The experience of trauma teaches us that there is a fragility at the heart of the fundamental assumptions on which the lives of each and every one of us are based. We defend what we perceive to be our core almost to the point of extinction, for the alternative is disintegration of the self. Our minds are capable of amazing feats of cognitive distortion in defence of our core assumptions. This is the common ground on which we all stand: paedophile, victim and bystander, every one of us is vulnerable.

Chapter 8

Into the black hole of trauma
the collapse of meaning

Look at my sleepless eyes, look at them. I never rest, or almost never. Day and night, I am alert, I hear things that others don't see, look at me ... I awake terrified, covered with sweat, as if I had died in my sleep. Dawn brings small comfort, for pain persists. But the light on the blue walls of my house in Coyoacán is so limpid, so clean, I must paint, I must live (*Frida Kahlo: The Camera Seduced*, Chronicle Books, 1992).

Art and literature and music have always been telling us the truths of trauma. Before there was science there were the stories of the horrors which may afflict us, the grief we must endure and the grace which may lift us beyond it. When science was silent, or silenced, still the stories were told. We know trauma, it is written in our bones as well as our brains.

My family were miners from Durham and Derbyshire and Cornwall, miners for as far back as generations of family bibles will take us; and the bibles hold the records: '1798, pit collapse, dead were Michael Hunter, Joseph Hunter, ...', six of them, my several greats grand-father and his young sons of whom the youngest was eight years old. I traced the names as a child, imagined the army of kin I would never have because these young ones did not live to reproduce. Knowing the silences, the things which are never said because they are too terrible to utter, the offspring of mining communities recognise trauma.

In the circles of harm and domains of silence generated by paedophilia tertiary victims are among the casualties. If we develop symptoms, and many of us do, then these will be symptoms of post traumatic stress; and if we develop a psychological disorder the diagnosis is likely to be

117

that we are suffering from post traumatic stress disorder. We have been measured against the criteria for diagnosis and found to have met them.

We have experienced, witnessed or been exposed to an event or events that involved actual or threatened death or serious injury, or a threat to the physical integrity of the self or others, and our response involved fear, helplessness, or horror. We have found ourselves suffering a range of symptoms which at a minimum include elements of both intrusion and avoidance, together with persistent symptoms of physiological arousal not present before the trauma; these symptoms cause significant distress or impairment in social, occupational, or other important areas of functioning, and persist over time.

People who are working in the field of paedophilia are pioneers, reaching out into new territory. Their mandate to explore is at best ambivalent. More sin-eater than saviour, they are likely to find themselves assigned to the role of pariah, the needed but despised cleaner up of detritus.

There is always a high casualty rate among pioneers. If the lessons are learned from their work, then the next to venture into the territory should have an easier time, and so onward until the new lands have become part of our ordinary world. Pariahs, on the other hand, will never be teachers; their prime function is to allow us not to learn the things we do not wish to know. If as a community we have any realistic commitment to protecting our children then it is important that we recognise workers in this field as pioneers and avoid consigning them to the status of pariahs. Then the suffering of the casualties will be worth something.

The possibility of defining as trauma what has happened to tertiary victims has been established. It is also clear that there are many reasons why the response to this exposure to trauma may be a sense of fear, helplessness or horror. If this primary criterion is met, what is it like to meet the other criteria for a diagnosis of post traumatic stress disorder? Weaving together my own experience with the stories I have heard provides some images, a typical day in the life of a tertiary victim organised to illustrate the criteria for a diagnosis of post traumatic stress disorder.

Daybreak: persistent intrusive re-experiencing

A working day may start at 3.00 a.m. or earlier. I have heard of a colleague similarly afflicted who wakes always at precisely 2.58, but I
have no such regularity in my life, only that perpetual waiting for the
telephone so that I never really feel that I have slept at all. Except that
I must have done, for how else explain the starting awake in such
terror? My heart has grown, it seems, while I lay asleep, and now it is
too big for the cavity of my chest, is pounding on my breastbone. I
think that I am dying. It is not possible to breathe, if I breathe my
bursting heart will have no space left at all and I will die.

After a few minutes the attack subsides and I can move. Lying down
will not help now. Once awake in these dead hours the scenes will
replay over and over until light comes. Or if I fall asleep the dreams
will come. I know that I am lucky, for at least I am not afraid of the
fear, can allow it to run its course and know that it is about my brain
playing tricks on the rest of my body. I have colleagues who are less
fortunate, who are, I can see, becoming more and more terrified of the
panic attacks. That way I know a short road to disaster lies, and no-
one seems to help them.

Work is a boundary, I would be lost without it. I have thought I should
do something else, that I have become a liability and not an asset, but
I am too old a dog to learn new tricks, and too stubborn to be forced
away from what I love. So I cling to my job, though basic skills have
gone.

I have lost the ability to write. Once, I remember, I wrote for fun and
led poetry workshops and when I woke in the night it was because I
had something waiting to be written. Then confidential reports were
leaked to the press, reports which I had written on the clear
understanding that I could be trusted with this very frightening
material. Now when I sit down to write I start to shake. There is a
place just under the hollow of my ribcage, just south and west of my
heart if a compass were drawn on my belly, which is where the
shaking starts.

I can write reports for work, as indeed I must, for this is my job. To
do it I must be in bed, which is my safe place never mind the nightmares. I need a hot water bottle for the cold which is a coldness deep

inside, causing me to shiver despite the thermometer which tells me it is summer. Propped up on pillows I can crouch, tigress in her lair – and never mind the rumours that lady is *scared* before she pounces – and I can, eventually, write a report.

So long as someone else is listening for the telephone, that is to say. Here's a pretty problem. I can write reports at home, but not in the office, but I can answer the telephone at the office but never at home. Which is not entirely true, of course. I do answer the telephone at home. To do so is a clear conscious process following the guidelines I have been taught: now stretch out hand and pick up the receiver, now hold it to the ear, now wait silently – legitimate callers will speak first to identify themselves. My friends mostly have stopped ringing, finding it too unnerving.

Breakfast is necessary. Food, once a delight to be savoured, has become fuel. I make myself eat enough despite the body's protests that it is busy trying to take care of this tight knot here in my middle and really cannot manage another mouthful. Some I know live through the day buying one another comfort treats, caretaking through calories, and becoming weightier by the day; others waste away before my eyes.

Today I will leave the newspaper on the mat for the others to read. I think I can remember a time when there was something else in the papers, but recently there has been so much news about child care and paedophilia that I have to be feeling strong to read the paper. Generally I turn to the back page and do the crossword. Snippets of reporting about football which surround it will not disturb my struggle for equilibrium, and I can rely on others in the household to tell me if there is anything happening I need to know about.

The walk to the garage is always an unnerving few yards. In my work with victims I have been assaulted, and I am told it may happen again, attachment making me a target of extreme emotions. I was advised to take lessons in self-defence, an interesting exercise. My expert tutor had a list of questions: Is your likely attacker bigger than you? Is he younger than you? Can he run faster than you? Is it likely that he will have been using alcohol or drugs? At the point of attack is he likely to be subject to internal inhibitors? To which the answers were: yes, yes, yes, yes, and no. There was a supplementary question: Do you have good life insurance?

I am aware of courage. It has taken form and substance for me. Watching the children play computer games I have noted how resources may be stored in a corner of the screen to be picked up as needed, and I have made myself parcels of courage, power balls set aside to get me through the day.

One to get me to the garage, one to open the garage and see what is inside, two more to get into the car. Three times now my car has been vandalised, twice while it was locked in the garage, and only my car damaged though my partner's car sits next to it. Now to get to my car I must turn off the garage alarm, undo three locks and still, knowing with certainty that it cannot have happened again since all these are intact, fight down the nausea as I open the garage door.

I liked my car. Silly, I know, but true. It used to feel like part of my home, an extension of the space in which I lived my life. Now it feels alien, spoiled, a constant reminder of dangerousness. Here is the groove where a screwdriver popped the window, there the marks left by prising out the door lock, and further back the reminders of the scrawled graffiti I scrubbed off sobbing.

On this bright day I wait for my guts to stop their churning and accept that, yes, I am going to spend the next forty minutes in the car, however much I may want not to be with these reminders. Driving to work is usually time out, the need to concentrate takes all my energy when my senses want to stray to every passing object and put it to the threat test. I have a friend who has a horse which is very brave, will tackle any jump, and never shies at passing juggernauts. Only one fear afflicts her, my friend tells me, this horse is afraid of tigers; there are great big tigers that hide behind trees, and little tiny tigers that hide under leaves, there are even cunning tigers that wait in telephone kiosks. If it weren't for the tigers this would be a safe world. My tigers have been snapping at my heels for months.

Cars are wonderful for hypervigilance. Here I have virtually three hundred and sixty degree visibility, I can be aware of so much more of my surroundings. I think perhaps I'll buy a hat with mirrors. There is behind me a black car with dark windows. My partner has noticed a car like this parked opposite the house four times this week, the driver never getting out; once it stayed for two hours before driving off.

Certainly it does not belong to any of the neighbours. My head says there are half a dozen explanations far removed from me: a boy in love with the neighbour's lovely daughter, somebody's bad debt collector, a scout for burglary, whatever. My stomach takes no notice of my head, but adds another layer to the knot which never leaves me for a moment.

Now I am fighting panic. White knuckle fear and 'where's the nearest house?' and 'can I reach my mobile phone?' and then I glance behind again to find the car has turned off, gone about its more or less innocent business. I can relax, then, which in this case means pull off the road, deposit my breakfast in the hedge, apologise to a slightly outraged cow, and after waiting for the shakes to stop drive on to work.

Morning: avoidance of stimuli associated with the trauma
I am, of course, a little late. Which means I may have missed the start of the meeting. Which means if I just take a few minutes to go to the toilet, sort out my desk, look at the post, get distracted by the notice board, and realise that in any case I have mislaid the agenda for the meeting, it will definitely be too late to be worth going in. Not that I have a problem with meetings; my supervisor asked me that and I was able to be completely reassuring on the subject. It is true that I did have some very bad experiences when all this was going on, meetings I take great care never to think about, but I can cope with that. Taking part in meetings is a central part of my work, and after more than twenty years of professional reliability I am well able to handle a few meetings where my professional integrity is attacked from unexpected quarters. Perfectly well able to handle it.

There are letters and memos I should have written last week. I think since there is now no point in going in to the meeting, I will make myself write these, my penance for being late. First I need a jug of water and a glass. My mouth is always dry these days, especially when I must sit and try to write without shaking too obviously. And I will need pain relievers for the ache across my neck. Thus set up, my morning will fill itself.

A lunch time gathering to say farewell to a colleague retiring from the residential sector is the next hurdle. More power balls of courage are needed to face it. Previously sociable and extravert, I find the loss of feelings of pleasure in the company of like-minded people indescribably painful. I know that I will sit there because it would be churlish not to go, and I will see people relating easily to one another, and it will be as though I had died inside. If it were not work related I would not go. At home I never go out now.

There is another dimension to the problem of being with a group of people from work. With my background and training I come from a generation which automatically, almost unconsciously, counts heads. How many women, how many men, how many black people, how many children, how many people with disability are there in this group? Now another head count automatically plays itself inside. How many paedophiles are here? Is it you? Or you?

Previously respected colleagues have been arrested, and I have never been able to play the game of ' I always thought there was something wrong with him.' I trusted and I felt my trust betrayed. At first I had thought that only men were involved, which at the time was bad news for my partner as I struggled to come to terms with what men were doing to children. Then, just when I had assimilated that, and grasped the truth that maleness was not the problem, I had to work with a situation in which the abuser was a woman, and start a whole new set of learning. Now I look round at my colleagues and I feel afraid. Whenever possible I will do something else rather than attend a social gathering from work.

Afternoon: autonomic hyperarousal

By mid-afternoon I have lost the plot. Since half way through the morning I have been craving caffeine and sugar, and through an afternoon on duty I have been filling the need with diet fizz and chocolate bars. The effect on a body addicted for twenty years to health foods and salad is electrifying. I could probably unplug my computer from the power supply and still keep it running from my excess useless energy.

I take a referral on a child suffering Attention Deficit Hyperactivity Disorder. Join the party, I think, as I go to look up a file reference, forget to do it and by the time I come back to my seat I've lost the notes I took about the case. Which means I must have left them down somewhere, in a building swarming with telephone engineers, and I am instantly distraught. These little daily things are now the acid in my soul. I was a good worker, and I cannot even take care of basic confidentiality for half an hour. Although I find the notes again, the damage is done, my self-confidence further undermined.

A friend rings from another agency, another part of the country, to say that the prosecution we had both been waiting for has fallen through. A year of work for several teams working in different areas, dozens of witnesses, and nothing to show for it. He sounds so flat he might have been on the wrong end of a steamroller; I know whatever I say will be meaningless, but say it anyway because I care.

My head is aching and I have taken my full quota of pain relief. I have two hours work left to do with only half an hour of working day; this has become normal for me, who used to be so quick and efficient, but now find simple tasks beyond me. I sit with a fresh cup of coffee and stare into space, waiting for the mounting rage to come under control by replacing it with emptiness. At last I hear the last person leave the office. I put my head down on the desk and howl, great tearing sobs that seem to be splitting me apart.

Now I can finish what I have to do in the peace of the empty office. Here I feel more secure than I do at home, it is the place of greatest safety for me short of being out of the country on holiday. Yet in the quiet of the evening I still jump to every sound. I have learned that, when startled, if I sit quietly and take my pulse this is the quickest way to settle my racing heart and distract myself from the fear. Picture of a madwoman, sitting alone and terrified in an empty office checking her pulse to make sure she has not yet died.

It is not possible for me to leave the office on time, I can no longer do a day's work in a working day. I travel home late again, the knot inside me tightening with every mile I cover as I anticipate the evening and the long hours of the night. I can remember feeling joyful. The space in my life which was filled with joy I experience as an amputation. I round a corner and am met by the sight of the sunset, I am embraced by colour; I know, and it grieves me to know, that once I would have been taken over by the surge of joy which waits on the discovery of such beauty.

Evening: impairment of social and occupational functioning

With every day that passes I am a little more destroyed by the loss of my professional abilities and the closing down of my responsiveness to the joy and delight in the world around me.

There is not one area of my life unaffected by the change. I am afraid of meeting people, they seem to me to be living in a different dimension of space and time. The world outside my skin and my inner world used to interlock smoothly and I lived my life with great joy, I remember. Now the world outside still looks as though it ought to be the same, but something in my inner world has slipped. The kaleidoscope has turned and I cannot make the inner patterns match the outer landscape. I am powerless on the other side of this disjunction.

At home I eat the meal my partner has prepared, because he has prepared it and not for pleasure in the food. And then ... ah yes, and then we spend an evening at home. Our life together has turned into an old joke: 'Do you remember how we used to spend our evenings at home?' 'I remember how. I can't remember why.'

We will set the intruder alarms in the garage and the house, and he will read a book and be there if I need him because I am one of the lucky ones and he will not give in and go away. I will smoke cigarettes, another innovation along with fizzy drinks and chocolate bars, which makes me feel a little better and which I know I will remember with astonishment if I ever emerge from this maze into the light again. And I will do crossword puzzles, or watch television without any idea of what is passing in front of my eyes, or sit and stare into space until enough time has passed and we go to bed.

Persistence over time

From the beginning to the end this was four years of my life. Some people work in the field of paedophile abuse and are not affected by it as traumatic stress. They suffer no injury. Some are affected but recover to a satisfactory level of functioning more quickly. Others never recover at all, or if they do recover are left with different but related chronic illnesses.

Those who do suffer post traumatic stress disorder and recover find that they and the world are transformed. Life on the other side of the black hole may seem outwardly the same, but when the person living the life has changed then everything is different.

When she was six years old, in 1913, Frida Kahlo suffered polio which resulted in her right leg being less developed than her left. She reacted to the deformity by making herself into a fine athlete, skating, swimming, boxing, and playing football. Twelve years later she was injured in a streetcar accident. She was impaled on a handrail, and suffered, as well as two fractured lumbar vertebrae, 'three fractures of the pelvis, eleven fractures of the right foot, dislocation of the right elbow, ... acute peritonitis ..' The next year she began to paint. Before she died at the age of forty seven she had undergone more than thirty two operations as a result of her accident and resulting complications. She married the artist Diego Rivera, twice, had love affairs, joined the communist party, wrote letters, and painted, and always painted. She was passionate and difficult and extraordinary, and she became a legend. While recovering from the accident she wrote to her boyfriend:

> If you knew how terrible it is to know suddenly, as if a bolt of lightning illuminated the earth. Now I live in a painful planet, transparent as ice; but it is as if I had learned everything in seconds. I became old in instants and everything today is bland and lucid. I know that nothing lies behind, if there were something I would see it. (Frida Kahlo: *The Camera Seduced*, Chronicle Books, 1992).

Chapter 9

The changed landscape
life after post traumatic stress disorder

Security is mostly a superstition. It does not exist in nature, nor do the children of men as a whole experience it. Avoiding danger is no safer in the long run than outright exposure. Life is either a daring adventure, or nothing (*The Open Door*, Helen Keller, 1957).

Traumatic stress is an injury which affects the physiological, psychological and social functioning of the victim. It is a systemic injury which requires a holistic response. We are changed by trauma physically, mentally, socially and spiritually, and in order to recover we must assimilate and adapt to the changes in all those dimensions of our being.

Physically we need to learn to control and manage the physiological responses which are generated initially by the trauma but which subsequently become a pattern for the interaction between self and environment. Psychologically we must be able to process the horrifying experience both cognitively and emotionally to the point where we have come to terms with it and it has become a painful but bearable memory. Socially we need to recover our links with those around us and rediscover our ability to make a difference in the world. Spiritually we need to reopen ourselves to the possibility of joy.

Sometimes we can make these adaptations spontaneously and recover. Sometimes we need help. The denial and repression of the recognition of trauma in our society, which is such a parable for the processes of denial and repression which occupy the energy of victims, have contributed to the development of social structures which do not lend themselves to the healing of trauma. We have a social order which actually and actively prevents us from treating people holistically.

Our existing structures for treating the wide range of symptoms and behaviours arising out of post traumatic stress disorder have been developed in a world of reductionist science, a world in which the tendency has been towards particularity and individuation. The emphasis has been on determining the existence of a condition which fits into the smallest diagnostic space available so that we can in a linear way apply a remedy to the identified problem and thus provide evidence that we have, or have not, cured it. That remedy will come from within the particular discipline of the practitioner whose expertise is being sought to resolve the identified problem. The problem will be seen as belonging to, being a property of, the individual identified as being in need.

Trauma is a small word, but it fills a very large diagnostic space. It extends beyond the bounds of the individual victim into the social order which provides the context both for the occurrence of the trauma and the recovery of those whom it affects. The problem which is trauma does not belong to any individual; it is not a property of the victim. Trauma is a property of human beings, it is intrinsic to the interplay between humanity and the environment in which we find ourselves.

In attempting to draw out treatment strategies in the real world, the world of our existing social structures, van der Kolk and colleagues have helpfully identified five phases of treatment which are needed for recovery. They acknowledge (p426) that the implied linear nature of such a process is artificial, that in reality this is a cyclical and almost certainly chaotic process. In a world still passionately attached to linear thinking it is temporarily helpful to place a static linear pattern over a truly chaotic process, so long as we remember that this static world we have imposed will itself crack and new patterns emerge out of new disorders as our understanding grows.

The five phases identified as necessary for recovery are:

- stabilization
- deconditioning of traumatic memories and responses
- restructuring of traumatic personal schemes

- re-establishment of secure social connections

- accumulation of restitutive emotional experiences

  (van der Kolk, McFarlane and van der Hart in van der Kolk *et al*, 1996, p426)

If this model has validity then tertiary victims who have recovered will be able to map the process of their recovery against it. Since it is a model which I believe is a helpful contribution to elucidating strategies for making space in our social structures to accommodate the realities of trauma, this seems a worthwhile exercise.

What is it like to have come through to the far side of the black hole of trauma? How does the world look when the pieces have been shaken up in the air and rearranged themselves? The experiences of tertiary victims of paedophilia will serve as examples. It would be possible to examine the recovery process for primary victims in a similar way, but it must be recognised that the desolation and devastation in the lives of children who have lived through organised sexual abuse is often so intense and so complex that this would be unrealistic. There is so great a need for further study and learning in this area. As for the experiences of secondary victims, this is almost uncharted territory. I hope that I have pointed to a field for research; I know that I have no knowledge of the subject other than knowing that the problem exists.

Stabilising

A safe space is a first necessity in recovering from traumatic stress. For many of the tertiary victims of organised and network child sexual abuse this seems an impossible requirement. One of the core assumptions to have been destroyed is the assumption that there are spaces free from the possibility of paedophilia. And there may be no physical safety; threats which may have been issued are not necessarily time limited. These workers have been involved in seriously spoiling the fun of people who are demonstrably willing to use violence themselves or to have others use violence on their behalf.

In reality all victims of trauma have passed beyond the illusion, the superstition, of safety. The world is not a safe place to live, and it is the only home we have. The creation of a safe space for recovery is just that: it is a creation of something out of nothing, the invention of a ground on which to stand, which for the time being will hold safe.

This safe ground is likely to be a therapeutic relationship. Under the impact of traumatic stress we are mazed, we do not know which way to turn. It is vital to have someone available who can see the way through the maze. Diagnostic categories generally do not help. To be told that we are suffering from depression or an anxiety state or whatever just does not seem to do justice to the range of thoughts and feelings which take us over when we are under the onslaught of traumatic stress.

Post traumatic stress disorder, if it is thoroughly explained to us, is different and helpful as a way of understanding what is happening to us. For as I have stated, and as Finkelhor (in Wyatt and Powell, 1988) complained, post traumatic stress disorder is a very wide category indeed – it fills a very large diagnostic space. This is precisely what the bewildered victim needs.

Drugs may be helpful in establishing a stable state from which the victim can begin the journey of recovery. The SSRI drugs look like being particularly helpful in targeting the overactive physiological responsiveness which prevents the victim from regaining control of their reactions or behaviour. My own experience with these drugs was that I hated them but they worked. The experience for me was of a sort of chemical lobotomy, a state in which I was conscious of a gap in my brain across which I could not make connections. Since the drugs did nothing to improve disrupted sleep patterns, I spent hours lying awake knowing that I was worried about something but not able to remember what it was. Nevertheless, the cycle had been broken, I was no longer triggered by every passing car or stray cat into startled terror, nor was I tormented by images of the destruction of my world, haunted by my own thoughts and physical responses.

Once the initial safety zone has been established, the remaining three elements of the process of stabilising can be summed up in the well-known election slogan: education, education, education.

It is crucial for the victim to learn about traumatic stress. We need to know what is happening to us, to become interested in the workings of our own mind-body instead of being terrified at our own un-controlled thoughts and feelings. I have found that victims seize eagerly on this information. The look of relief on the face of someone who is discovering that their craziness makes sense in the context of traumatic stress reminds me of the look I would expect to see on the face of a person drowning who has just been thrown a lifeline. In my own case I had the advantage that I already knew about traumatic stress; the knowledge did not stop me becoming a victim, but it did mean I never became afraid of the experience itself.

We need to relearn the language of feelings. Traumatic stress removes the capacity to express feelings in words. It is a fact of the way our brains function that for us humans the flow of emotion which accom-panies a stimulus is blocked until we can assign a symbol to it. We are creatures of narrative memory, condemned to replay experiences end-lessly unless and until we can consign them to their place in the story of our life. After traumatic stress we have to relearn how to represent feelings symbolically, usually by recovering the words and reconnect-ing them to the feeling.

The others in our social network also need to be educated about trauma. Since traumatic stress is a social phenomenon, we cannot establish a safe ground for our recovery until the people around us are aware of our needs and not afraid of our transformation. Rosencrantz and Guildenstern failed miserably in their efforts to grasp what troubled Hamlet despite being specifically charged to 'glean what afflicts him'. Just a little education in the effects of having the core assumptions of our lives shattered might have given these two early diagnosticians some insight into the ghosts which haunted Hamlet, and saved so much tragedy!

Deconditioning the memories

The processing of the traumatic memory fragments to relegate the traumatic events to their place in narrative memory is essential to the process of recovery. Discerning effective therapeutic interventions to help people with this activity is a puzzle, however.

Post traumatic stress disorder is a very broad diagnosis, and growing all the time as we are learning more about the full range of experiences which may give rise to traumatic stress. This is appropriate, for we have needed a way to describe the results of an injury which causes the collapse of our deep cognitive structures. It is not a way of inventing fashionable new illnesses, but rather a means of giving us at last the scope to reclassify as recognisable injury a host of disorders which in the past have disabled many lives but remained beyond our understanding. Our map of the world of the human psyche has for a long time had large areas designated simply 'here be dragons', the great unknown tracts of 'personality disorders', 'conduct disorders' and all the other areas defined as both dangerous and unknowable (see Carter, 1998, p8).

Our therapeutic tools have been built to correspond to the needs of the territory as it existed on our maps. They have also been created in the environment of a reductionist science. When the belief is that a person 'has' a condition for which we may provide a cure, then the competing therapeutic approaches will be assessed against their success in curing that condition. Post traumatic stress disorder, by contrast, is not a condition but a complex and persistent bio-psycho-social response to an experience which a complex organism has so far been unable to assimilate. Now we need a new approach to assessing the success or failure of various techniques which may be of service to different persons in different social settings at different stages of the disorder.

What this potentially large range of therapies will have in common is their usefulness in reducing symptoms of disorder and increasing indicators of integration and adaptation. This is the dawning of a genuinely holistic approach to treatment. Many different stressors may result in traumatic stress, many different factors lead from the experience of traumatic stress to the development of post traumatic stress disorder, and the disorder will express itself differently in each unique constellation of person-in-their-social-network which is the location of the meaning world which has collapsed.

Effective therapy will therefore be dependent not on having the right stock prescription, but on having the skill to assess the needs of this constellation which is presented to us as an individual person but is in reality part of a system which is in disorder as a result of traumatic stress. There will also need to be a recognition that the phenomenon of resistance to therapeutic intervention is not a problem in the treatment of post traumatic stress disorder but is actually part of the solution. The victim has survived the traumatic stress because they have been able to resist being destroyed by the horror; effective therapeutic strategies will need to utilise the victim's own ability to defend themselves from total disintegration whilst providing new possibilities for integration and adaptation.

Deconditioning of traumatic memories and responses may be helped by cognitive emotional education (Bob Johnson), cognitive behavioural therapy, drug therapy, systematic desensitization, imaginal flooding, biofeedback, prolonged exposure, stress inoculation therapy, eye movement desensitization and reprocessing (a technique drawn from neuro-linguistic-programming), visual-kinesthetic dissociation (also from NLP), non-directive hypnosis, implosion therapy, and a range of other therapies which currently exist as well as many others will surely be invented as we gain a better understanding of the subject.

Therapeutic techniques will be counter productive if they generate reminders or memories of the trauma without having in place strategies for the victim to develop control of the powerful physiological responses which will be involved. They will be dangerous if they do not provide a safe environment in which to allow the process of deconditioning to be contained. And they will be ineffective if they provide nothing but talk; victims of post traumatic stress disorder need to be able to be actively involved in their own recovery, to be able to create meaningful symbols for the reinvention of meaning.

Such powerful symbolic activities as learning a new skill, changing their physical appearance, writing to or otherwise confronting their abuser, burning symbolic representations of the past, keeping a journal, may all serve to bridge the gap between thought and feeling and the physical world which has become so muddled for the victim of post traumatic stress disorder.

Reconstructing the foundations

With the exception perhaps of some practitioners of Zen, people cannot contain a cognitive vacuum. When traumatic stress instantaneously deconstructs fundamental cognitive schemas the mind instantaneously begins to construct alternatives. These traumatic personal schemes then feed into the maintenance of the post traumatic stress disorder, for they naturally take account of, and provide a meaning structure for, the trauma which has become the central organising principle of life for the victim.

People who believe that 'I am the sort of person to whom bad things happen' or 'It is dangerous for me to be happy' or 'I am a source of contamination in the world, harming those around me' are unlikely to live a happy life or win friends and influence people. Assisting victims to restructure these traumatic personal schemes is a central task of therapy in post traumatic stress disorder.

Tertiary victims of paedophilia will similarly have struggled to develop a way of understanding their changed world. The range of issues around which core constructs have collapsed may include: trust, safety, authority, power, social and political structures, gender and sexuality, professional competence, personal courage and resilience, personal effectiveness, religious faith, and personal and social relationships. Constructs based on the terror and helplessness of trauma will have replaced any previous constructs which have dissolved. Victims need help to challenge these cognitive constructs and to develop new schemes which take account of the changed reality but also allow for a full and satisfying life to be lived.

Again there will be no one right way of providing these therapeutic interventions. The crucial factors are likely to be the provision of a safe space and a trustworthy relationship within which the challenges to our new common sense can be accepted and the possibilities of cognitive creativity explored. A space and a relationship which take full account of the unique person-in-a-social-context which we call a self, and which is at any given time the sum of the life we have lived until now and the life we have the potential to live in the future.

Rebuilding connections
It is of critical importance to tertiary victims of paedophilia to be able to re-establish secure social connections and to rebuild a sense of personal and interpersonal efficacy. The sense of betrayal and the dis-

solution of trust which are characteristic of this victimization, the impact on personal, sexual, and social relationships, the onslaught on personal and professional confidence and effectiveness, all play a major part in the collapse of the central constructs of meaning which lead to the development of post traumatic stress disorder.

The creation of peer groups of support may be of great value here. Just as survivor groups can be beneficial for those recovering from disasters and from specific traumatic events such as rape and child abuse, so support groups both within professional settings and across agency boundaries can be wonderfully regenerative of a sense of meaning and purpose.

Children who have suffered trauma often need help to create 'cover stories' for themselves. These are ways of telling enough of the truth about themselves to enable them to participate in social settings, without creating alienating discomfort in others by disclosing truths which the others are not prepared to hear. Tertiary victims will have been socially competent people, but this does not necessarily make it easier to re-establish social relationships during recovery. Often the experience of being unable to make adequate contact, the loss of easy social conversation, the loss of a voice socially as well as professionally, may be additionally disabling for people whose sense of self is thus further fractured. In these circumstances recovering victims may need their own versions of cover stories, opportunities to rehearse ordinary social interchange.

There are many other possibilities which may be explored on the journey through to the far side of trauma. Keeping a journal, writing letters, joining new social groups, learning some new skill, experimenting in all sorts of ways with the boundaries of the self emerging from the chaos, will all contribute to the creation and recreation of social connectedness and personal power.

Accumulating restitutive experience

For the recovery to be complete it must be possible to live a rich and personally satisfying life after post traumatic stress disorder. One of the most distressing features of the disorder when it persists over time is anhedonia, the loss of the capacity to experience joy. This is an extension of the initial protective numbing which shields the victim at the point of traumatic stress from being totally disintegrated by the force of the collapse. The numbing is very persistent and is not identical to depression, which may also be present.

It is an essential for the recovering victim to have access to a wide range of joyful, pleasurable and satisfying experiences. These may be, for example:

- Physical: sports, massage, making love, walking the dog, dancing

- Intellectual: reading, studying, doing crossword puzzles, writing

- Aesthetic: painting, visiting exhibitions, making music, listening to music

- Practical: gardening, building, cooking, craft work

- Spiritual: meditation, prayer, religious ceremonies, shared worship.

The only limits are those of the imagination and the purse, but everyone should be able to find activities which would delight them if only they were not suffering from anhedonia. As they make progress in recovering from the disorder they will begin to notice that they can take pleasure again in the life which flows through them. Then it is important for them to take on the task of recognising and naming the resurrection of joy in themselves. This gives the victims a way of tracking their own recovery which is delightful in itself and which re-awakens in them the language and symbolism of delight.

For me, to nurse a grandchild and feel nothing was exquisite torture, made no easier to bear by the knowledge that there was no torturer other than my own disordered mind. And life then was a daily round of such tortures, for I had been used to living with a keen appreciation of the joyfulness of ordinary things. On the other hand, the recovery of the experience of joy was a return to Eden, a gift of 'light on the blue walls of my house' which was enough in itself to make me declare, as Frida Kahlo did, 'I must live.'

Transformation

The world is changed for those of us who have been fortunate enough to be safely held while we traversed the wasteland. We who have been sustained by some combination of the network of close relationships, good friendships, sound and effective therapy, professional support, religious faith, moral principles and personal resilience, which can provide the ground on which we may stand while we discover who we have become. A different ground for each one of us, as we are different from one another, and a different journey of discovery, for the collapse into chaos is not the same experience for any two people.

At the other end of that journey, according to Tedeschi and Calhoun (1995), is transformation. It is common for survivors to reach a point of valuing what has happened to them. This is not a prescriptive valuing; there is no belief in survivors that it would be a good thing for others to go through what they have experienced. It is more of an existential valuing, a sense that they have learned and grown through the experience, that they are now different persons and in some way better. The horror and the terror are not valued, but the learning and personal growth which they have generated are.

This might be seen to be another illusion, another construct based on the need for positive bias. Indeed it may be. But there is reporting from many observers of changes after extreme suffering of this kind which include a movement towards serenity and creativity. People do not only report of themselves that they feel more serene and lucid and creative, they are also seen that way by others around them.

Survivors would in any case be unlikely to worry about the illusory nature of their sense of well-being. For they have first hand knowledge of the fragility of our assumptions and cognitive schemes. Having been compelled to recognise that security is nothing but superstition and all safety an illusion, they may experience the excitement of the daring adventure which the rest of their uncertain life may become.

> Are there doors? There is earth and within us the earth creates time and time within us thinks and is buried,
>
> but – pointing to the Babylonian constellations – we can contemplate this world and the others and delight in them,
>
> and contemplation opens other doors: it is a transfiguration and a reconciliation,

we can laugh at the monsters and smile at the iniquities with the smile of Pyrrho or Christ,

they are different but the smile is the same, there are invisible passageways between doubt and faith,

freedom is to say *forever* when we say *now*, it is an oath and it is the art of the transparent enigma:

it is the smile – and it unchains the prisoner, says no to the monstrous, says yes to the sun of this moment, freedom is

– and you never finished: you smiled and drank your whiskey. The waters of the dawn washed out the constellations.

Man is his visions.

(Kostas Papaioannou (1925-1981), Octavio Paz, *The Collected Poems, 1957-1987* (Weinberger, 1991)

Chapter 10

Issues
victims, organisations and society

Lift up your faces, you have a piercing need
For this bright morning dawning for you.
History, despite its wrenching pain,
Cannot be unlived, but if faced
With courage, need not be lived again.

'On the Pulse of Morning', Maya Angelou,
(*The Complete Collected Poems*, 1995)

Paedophilia generates circles of harm which have caused damage throughout the entire social order which sustains us. The patterns of denial and minimisation, alternating with horror and outrage, which make up our communal response to organised child sexual abuse, are mirror images of the cycles of intrusion and avoidance which wreak such havoc in the lives of primary victims.

It is as though entire societies need to cure themselves of thinking which is based around traumatic memories and constructs. Like Freud in his time, we begin to grasp an idea and then, as the implications start to dawn on us, the idea and everything connected with it is inexorably repressed and denied. What would happen if we allowed ourselves to be cured? We would move through the phases of recovery:

Stabilization
First we need to create zones of safety, areas in which we can debate openly and clearly the issues as they arise, without the debates being subverted by our own denial and avoidance or by the cognitive distortions of the paedophiles among us. Given that we do not know

which of us are paedophiles, and that by definition we do not recognise our own avoidance, this is in itself a tall order. If we give way to the dynamics of helplessness which so powerfully attach themselves to paedophilia we shall never make the changes we must make for the sake of the children, however, so it will be worth trying to establish the settings in which we can debate fearlessly.

Education is the next step in the process of stabilization. We need to learn about trauma, traumatic stress, post traumatic stress disorder, and the traumagenic nature of paedophilia. We also need to learn to stop thinking and feeling with our guts and start thinking with our heads and feeling with our hearts. That is to say we need to separate out the inchoate jumble of somatic sensations and automatic thoughts which afflict us when confronted with paedophile abuse into a language of feelings and rational thinking.

The reaction of many people to the thought of paedophilia is 'It makes me feel sick', and there is that gesture to the solar plexus, or 'I'd like to kill (castrate, kick, whatever) them all', and a look of intense rage fleetingly crosses the features. There is a widespread inability to express feelings about paedophilia in words, although there is no such complete impoverishment of language with regard to most other crimes, even horrific crimes.

This response is not confined to any particular group of people but seems to be quite general. I believe, moreover, that there are professionals in the field who have such a response to paedophilia but suppress it in order to do the work. The result seems to be a language which is often intellectually adequate but impoverished in affect. We do not need to wallow in feelings, indeed we need not to do so, but we do need to reflect in the language we use that we are dealing with broken bodies and broken lives. We need to learn and relearn appropriate words for appropriate feelings.

Deconditioning of automatic responses

Once we discover a language in which we can talk about paedophilia appropriately it can then become a domain of discourse instead of a domain of silence. This would provide the basis for moving beyond those conditioned responses which are our communal equivalent of the trauma conditioned responses of victims. Allowing ourselves to think the unthinkable, we begin to detach from the instantaneous and unthinking reaction that prevents us from engaging rationality on the subject.

There is no need to extend the metaphor. It is essential that we develop the ability to look levelly and rationally at just what it is that paedophiles do to children, and what we must do in response.

Reconstructing the foundations

There is an urgent need to develop new shared beliefs about paedophilia and the effects of organised and network child sexual abuse. At the moment our existing common cognitive constructs are opaque to us, because we have not reached this phase of recovery, but there seem to be elements of believing that we are helpless, believing that paedophiles are monsters (rather than people who do monstrous things), believing that paedophiles are powerful and dangerous, believing that victims are different from ordinary children, and believing that thinking about these things will damage us.

Changing inaccurate schemas is painful and difficult work. It will only happen if we allow it to be an incremental process for which the energy and motivation are generated by refusing to continue to avoid hearing. We would then be able to hear the voices of victims and the silent screams of those who can only tell us through their behaviour of the torture they have suffered.

Rebuilding the connections

If we could stop seesawing from avoidance to intrusion, establish paedophilia as a domain of discourse, and restructure the cognitive categories available to us for thinking about paedophile abuse and its effects, then we would begin to be able to care for one another effectively.

The political will to address the needs we would then be able to identify will not be present until enough of us are able to do these things enough of the time. Once that critical point is reached it will happen, for we will discover that it simply begins to make sense. Our common sense view of the world will have shifted.

Once resources are made available, which follows on the changing of the political will, we would be presented with a set of solvable problems around ways and means. Social connections could then be built based on secure foundations instead of the horrifying shifting sands which now confront anyone who tries to work in this field. Victims, their families and carers, and workers in the field would then be safely held in a social network which at last could tolerate the realities of organised child sexual abuse.

'As if ...' says a voice in my head.

Blake Morrison wrote an extraordinary, moving and haunting book after attending the trial of the young boys who killed the toddler James Bulger. He called the book 'As If', and in it he recounts among other things the journey from journalistic curiosity to obsession. The experience forces him to confront the whole question of the way we construct childhood, all the issues of innocence and guilt, responsibility and moral accountability, which proved so difficult for all of us to think about sensibly at the time. In the end he is left with fantasies, of alternative endings to the original crime, and of alternative societies in which such events would be construed differently.

I feel ashamed of my fantasies. They're inappropriate, I know. I'm a bundle of inappropriateness, a night-wandering man pierced with the remembrance of a grievous wrong (Morrison, 1997, p237).

Yet there really is no 'as if' about it. We can change the way we think about childhood and the things that happen to children and the things that children do. Historically our community has made changes just as great in its shared thinking. It takes time and patience and energy but it does happen. Then we re-establish our social connections, and the changes we have made mean that in reality this is an entirely new version of social connectedness.

The first steps are to recognise the issues as they appear to the various people involved. This is an exercise we really need to do gathered together in groups, sharing ideas, growing the energy together to make things happen. All I can do at this stage is to offer suggestions as to what some of those issues might be and some of the implications of paying attention to the issues.

Victim issues

Victims need to be recognised and they need a response. The major issues for all the various victims of paedophilia centre on these two needs, to gain recognition and to elicit an appropriate response.

Primary victims, the children who are abused by paedophiles, need us to notice them. This is not as easy as it might sound, for we may reasonably guess that most of them are not telling us what has happened to them. Silenced, robbed of a voice to speak the horror clearly, they act out through their behaviour the pain which consumes them. It is a group of children in need which is almost impossible to quantify. We cannot grasp the extent of the need let alone gather an assessment of the nature of it.

We do know that there are many different versions of being a primary victim. The range extends from the child abused in a family with a culture of paedophilia, through children abused by lone paedophiles outside the family, children assaulted by 'predatory' paedophiles, children abused while in institutional care, and children abused by organised abuse networks, to children fully absorbed into an underworld culture of child prostitution and child pornography.

All these children need us to recognise what is happening to them. Most of them, we guess from the reports we receive from adults of their victimisation as children, will not tell us. They may be silenced by threats, by coercion, by traumatic amnesia, or by their own lack of language. Those who do not tell us in words, however, will almost certainly be telling us through their behaviour that they are being systematically destroyed. They need us to have ears to hear and eyes to notice the pain being acted out in front of us. And they need us to have a social order which does not reject what they have to communicate so emphatically that, rather than accept the unacceptable reality, it will make secondary and tertiary victims of those who do hear and notice the pain of the victims.

After recognition, response. The issues which primary victims have to bring before us in relation to the response we make to the injury we have recognised are numerous and weighty. The experience of many victims is that we could not have got our response much more wrong even if we had sat down and planned to make a mess of it.

Victims of post traumatic stress disorder need stability, therapy, secure social attachments and the possibility of joy. They do not need long drawn out criminal investigations (we might, but they don't). They do not need to be moved from an abusive home to an abusive institution, to be shifted around from one placement to another, to be left in a loving home but with no support provided, to find that no-one can contain their disordered behaviour, to be classified as criminal themselves, to be excluded from school, to be stuck in the middle of arguments over funding, or any of the hundred and one other things we can subject them to in our attempts to manage the situation within the limits of our understanding and resources.

It is characteristic of post traumatic stress disorder that it persists over time. Victims are likely to have needs lasting over many years. There may be a continuation of the same set of needs as symptoms persist, or there may be new needs arising as the processes of maturation changes the manifestation but not the condition. In either case our current services are not answering the needs. NAPAC, the National Association for People Abused in Childhood, has been set up in the last few years to draw attention to the unmet needs of adults who were victims of abuse as children. They also hope to create an information bank of resources.

Adult surviving victims of paedophilia often become serial service users when they grow up, as their complex and unrecognised disorder produces chaos in various aspects of their personal and social functioning. Symptoms may persist unchanged and affect a number of areas of life, or the presenting symptoms may change as the disorder manifests itself differently in the maturing victim.

People will continue to experience physical, emotional, mental, and behavioural symptoms from the original trauma. It is also in the nature of trauma that victims are likely to be retraumatized. They may harm themselves or they may place themselves in settings where they will be harmed; this is a familiar feature of the disorder arising out of the trauma related cognitive constructs which are all the mazed victim has available as guides to living.

The fragmentation of the self continues to be reflected in the services we offer to victims. One person living out the horror of post traumatic stress disorder amongst us may find themselves on the case books of the health service, the social services department, housing agencies, probation, the police, drug and alcohol services, welfare agencies, counselling services, relationship guidance services and employment services, sometimes all at the same time. This is a serious issue for people whose difficulties partly arise from their inability to discover or create an integrated sense of self, who daily suffer the pains of disintegration.

Secondary victims, the non-abusing families of, or carers for, victims also need recognition. This is a seriously neglected group of people. The pressure of day to day life with children who have suffered organised child sexual abuse is intense, and beyond imagining for most people who have not experienced it. The symptomatic behaviours which the children present day by day and hour by hour have a sort of toxic synergy. Any one manifestation by itself may be readily tolerated once we understand what is going on, but the relentless pressure of the whole being greater than the sum of the parts is often intolerable.

Carers commonly develop symptoms themselves, and may in particularly adverse circumstances develop post traumatic stress disorder. This secondary victimization is preventable. If carers are taught about traumatic stress, encouraged to notice early signs in themselves and provided with resources to take pre-emptive action, they will probably not develop disorder. Support groups help, peer support helps, respite care helps, promoting and encouraging self-care and relaxation, learning strategies for managing post traumatic disordered behaviour, learning how to teach affective language in daily care, these all help. Instead families who are often blaming themselves for the fact that their child was abused are further stigmatized by being seen as failing to cope.

Foster families may also find their own children developing symptoms as they live with the daily struggles of the primary victims. There is a curious ambivalence in agencies towards fostering families, which can manifest itself in these circumstances. They are admired for what they do, and it is recognised as an essential service without which we could not run our child care systems in this country. Yet if their own children begin to develop signs of stress, or even indicators of traumatic stress, the parents are then given strong if usually non-verbal messages that they are culpable for subjecting their children to this stress. This is a story I have heard repeatedly from carers, and have observed from within agencies. There is a real reluctance to recognise the burdens we place on children who foster.

If carers do fall victim to secondary traumatic stress and develop disabling symptoms then the disorder is treatable. Treatment depends on diagnosis, however, and most carers who develop post traumatic symptoms will in practice find themselves being treated for some other condition. This is likely to help part of the problem, leaving the other parts to get worse. Treatment for depression, for example, will do nothing about the panic attacks, whilst treating the anxiety may leave the deep depression untouched, and so on.

We can see that again the pressing issues are of recognition and response. The need to be noticed and have our situation assessed accurately, and the need to elicit an appropriate response from the social and political environment in which we find ourselves.

Tertiary victims are likely to raise very similar issues. They also need recognition and a response. In a precisely similar way, the recognition must be accurate and not stigmatizing, and the response must deal with the total spread of the symptoms and not just a diagnostically convenient or acceptable portion.

It is likely that tertiary victimization is entirely preventable once we have learned how to prevent it, although there may still be situations in which specific vulnerabilities are activated in workers. Training and preparation are wonderful protectors against traumatic stress for staff in occupational groups likely to be exposed to toxins.

The issue here is ensuring that the training of staff deals not only with the established professional issues but also provides information about and rehearsal for the particularly toxic nature of work in the field of paedophilia. This means that workers need to plan and rehearse for the real life experiences of the pervasiveness and hiddenness of paedophilia in just those professions which will be concerned with investigating the crimes and caring for the victims. It also involves preparing for the ways in which organised and network child sexual abuse impacts on personal, professional, and organisational areas of vulnerability.

Support structures need to be appropriate to the special toxicity of this field. Peer support is vital. So is 'grief leadership' (Ursano, Grieger and McCarroll in van der Kolk et al, 1996, p452), a style of management in which the leader remains congruent and supportive of feelings as well as ensuring task completion, even when the feelings are intensely difficult. Informal support structures need to be formally recognised in toxic work; partners and close kin will be carrying a heavy burden, and there should be plans to acknowledge that and to provide training and support if appropriate. Agency management structures should have absorbed the information about the toxicity of this work and the needs of workers involved in it, and have made advance plans to ensure the well-being of staff.

There is also a need for external consultancy and monitoring which is available to workers in all the agencies involved. This is both a preventive measure, since external consultancy is vital in systemic working at this level of toxicity, and a route to effective treatment for staff who develop symptoms. External consultants can also provide the debriefing which staff and management will need.

Organisational issues

Just as paedophilia presents profound challenges to the fundamental assumptions of individuals, generating traumatic stress and injuries or provoking avoidance and denial as a defence against such injury, so it shakes organisational assumptions to their foundations. The result is that all the agencies exhibit their own cognitive distortions in connection with organised child sexual abuse.

Cognitive distortions are real mote and beam issues; we can easily see the mote of dust distorting the vision of other people but have no way of seeing the great plank of wood in our own eye. When we bear in mind that agencies which suffer organisational cognitive distortion are made up of individuals each of whom has their own ways of viewing the world through distorting lenses, then we can begin to discern the complexity of the issues which face organisations trying to sort themselves out to deal with organised child sexual abuse.

The first great hurdles are denial and avoidance. These will yield only to steady, persistent, relentless pressure through education. And since these are actually about psychic defences and not about ignorance, the educators should never be discouraged by lack of progress. Learning in such areas is very sudden and very rapid; it has an astonishing all-or-nothing quality to it – one day we are talking nonsense, the next we are delivering the same old thing that everybody knows, and no recognition that any learning has taken place in between the two.

Then there are the workers and managers who are paedophiles and who have a negative influence on organisational learning in this field. Since we will make stringent efforts to avoid witch hunts it will not do to try to guess who. Instead we must make every effort to ensure that we have systems in place which make it, as far as we are able, impossible for children to be abused by them, carry on steadily educating the whole staff group, and wait for them to go away. There should be a big warning notice at this point: denial and avoidance in this field do not imply guilt, whether it is denial of personal involvement or denial that a manifest problem actually exists. It is dangerous for us to give in to the temptation to make guesses about paedophilia. We can make no reliable guesses about the sexual behaviour, feelings and fantasies of other people, ever.

The restrictions imposed by the purpose and structure of the agencies within which we work can also define the cognitive categories within which we can think about organised child sexual abuse. It is obvious that the police think about paedophilia as a crime or series of crimes, that social services departments think about it as a set of issues in working with children and families, that health agencies think about issues in physical and mental health of patients, that education agencies think about running schools and issues of learning and behaviour and, to come almost full circle, that justice agencies think about offenders.

Post traumatic stress disorder lends itself, under our current professional systems, to being split up into bits. It produces such a bewildering range of symptoms that it can easily satisfy the definitions of service need of half a dozen service providing agencies at the same time. One lone child may at the same time be a victim of crime and witness for the prosecution, a child on the at-risk register or being looked after in the care of the local authority, presenting a range of clinical symptoms, exhibiting emotional, behavioural and learning difficulties at school, be running amok in the community with offending behaviour, and be the precipitating cause of marital problems in the family home.

It is the legacy of our reductionist past that we focus on that range of symptoms which lie within our own professional discipline and fail to notice or ascribe meaning to the rest. From the point of view of the victim of post traumatic stress disorder there really is no hierarchy of symptoms. All the symptoms are reactions to or escapes from the pervading terror. The nightmare which woke us, the panic attack which stopped us going back to sleep, the towering rage we got into at breakfast time, the forgetfulness which made us overlook homework, the diarrhoea during the morning, the blind lashing out at an acquaintance in the afternoon, and the stealing a bottle of vodka on the way home and drinking to oblivion, are all from the perspective of the victim the same phenomenon. Yet that one set of symptomatic experiences could attract the attention of practitioners from five different agencies, each of whom will construe the event or behaviour in a different way.

Under these conditions, and they are common in this field of work, organisations which think solely within the boundaries of the service definitions of their own agency may contribute to the fragmentation which is the chief result of, and the most devastating injury to arise from, organised child sexual abuse. The need to develop genuinely holistic service provision in response to paedophile abuse is very pressing.

There will also be significant issues of liaison between all these agencies which will need to be approached with creativity and openness. Once we realise that we can contribute to the perpetuation of the post traumatic stress disorder which is so devastating the life of the child, we should all find a strong motivation to move beyond our own narrow professional boundaries. It will take great efforts on the part of all the organisations, but some efforts are well worth the making.

Every agency involved will have organisational problems with funding and resources for this work. Paedophilia generates some of the most expensive work undertaken in any of the agencies concerned. Until there is a real political will throughout the social order to do the work and do it thoroughly, these problems will remain and will be an issue. The political will cannot be created until we have come to a full appreciation of the true cost of failing to do the work. Even then it will take some upheaval of our existing structures to do it adequately; but it can be done, and therefore in the end it must be done. We shall have to find a way.

Social issues

The issue of the need to address the denial and avoidance, as well as the cognitive distortions which attach themselves to paedophilia, has already been noted. There is a broadly educative process perceptible in much modern literature, drama, and work for television.

The search for explanations of adult disordered behaviour in the experiences of the child has been an almost universal theme in recent years. It has been echoed even in news reporting in the tabloid press as well as the broadsheets; pages devoted to the horrific childhood experiences of murderers, whose crimes have been viewed with odium, are a quite recent phenomenon. It is beginning to be received wisdom that people who do really terrible things as adults must have had a really terrible childhood. These were still relatively revolutionary thoughts when Bob Johnson was writing in *The Guardian* only a few years ago.

There is, of course, a long way still to go. And the operation of the forces of repression, avoidance and denial leads to a situation in which people can easily hold completely contradictory thoughts at the same time. Thus it is possible for people to believe that someone is an inhuman monster who, at the very least, should be locked up forever and the key thrown away, and at the same time be aware of them as a hurt, deprived and abused child.

It is beginning to look a little more hopeful that we can reach a shared understanding at some level that children who have been victims of paedophilia may develop behaviour patterns which are socially unacceptable and personally harmful. I see no sign that we are any closer to a recognition of the nature of paedophilia or an understanding that paedophiles are not bizarre aliens whom we could easily pick out at a distance of half a mile.

The same phenomena that apply to workers in thinking about paedophilia apply to the rest of the population – only more so. The internal and external inhibitors against sexual activity with children are strong, the taboo is for most people powerful and effective. So effective that it becomes very difficult to think about people who have crossed it. Denial is as strong as the taboo.

It is also certain, on the basis of what we now know, that there will be an unknown proportion of the adult population who were themselves abused by paedophiles as children and who have traumatic amnesia for the event. For these people strong denial will be doubly strengthened, for they will face the terror of disintegration if they force themselves to confront facts which may trigger the trauma.

Thus the existence of paedophiles is denied. Or rather, since it is clear that paedophiles do exist, their existence is believed to be elsewhere, a sort of extended version of the not-in-my-backyard phenomenon. And they are demonized, made to be alien, other, not like us. The thought that paedophiles are living, breathing, feeling human beings who may live ordinary lives as our next door neighbours, except that their particular distortions of thought and feeling both compel and allow them to relate to children as sex objects, is generally repressed. Our cognitive and affective distortions hide from us our neighbours, colleagues, friends, kinfolk and people in authority over us whose secret behaviour, generated and sustained by their own cognitive and affective distortions, is hurting children.

This will take us some time to unravel. The avoidance and denial which surround paedophilia are serious issues. Which are compounded, of course, by the vested interest paedophiles have in persuading us that they do no exist. The extraordinary smokescreens of misinformation and disinformation, distortions and lies, which are put out by paedophiles as cover and justification make fantastic reading. They remind me of the old insurance company story: 'I wasn't there, and I wasn't drunk, and anyway the bed was on fire when I got into it.'

Denial, avoidance and repression also apply to thinking about trauma, traumatic stress and post traumatic stress disorder. It is very hard for us to confront our own fragility unless we have to. So long as we can consign victims of post traumatic stress disorder to some category of otherness it is possible to avoid noticing that they and we are similarly vulnerable. We have seen that this has been a very powerful dynamic in the denial of the devastation which actually is all around us and plain to see. It remains a serious issue in our attempts to move forward to the day when all the victims of organised child sexual abuse may reach recovery.

Systemic problems need systemic solutions. In the end the problems of providing a holistic response to the needs of victims of post traumatic stress disorder in general, and the effects of organised and network child sexual abuse in particular, will be part of a move towards a radical restructuring of the services we provide. A holistic response is the only meaningful and effective response, in terms of both prevention and treatment.

The issue, then, is one of political will. We have the ability and the technology now. We have moved beyond the days of linear thinking, and we are able as a community to produce systemic thinking of considerable sophistication. We could design programmes of action which would provide a powerful strategic approach to preventing and treating the effects of paedophilia. The question is, do we want to?

All systemic strategic planning will contain circularities. We need research which will show us whether it is really worth our while as a community to bother investing time, energy and resources to solving the problems. At the same time we need that research to be designed holistically, bearing in mind the new paradigms indicating that research is never a detached and objective activity, that the research act is also a part of the system activity (e.g. Reason and Rowan, 1981). We need interim investigative, preventive and therapeutic activities which are themselves strategically co-ordinated. And finally, and here is the circularity, we need research evidence on each step of the way, so that we can assess the effectiveness of various strategic interventions if we do decide that this is where we should be investing our money as a community.

It is a hard thought that we might look at so much suffering of such intensity and decide that we are not going to provide the resources needed to make it better. Yet these are the decisions we have to make all the time. It is vital, however, that we do so on the basis of informed understanding and not on the current basis of widespread avoidance and denial.

If the informed choice is that we cannot afford the resources we would need to make a genuinely holistic and systemic response to the prevention, investigation and treatment of the effects of organised and network child sexual abuse, then workers and managers in the various agencies which pick up the pieces will need to plan to work together on integrated strategic programmes so far as budgets and staffing will allow. An extension of the sort of interim strategic planning which currently goes on wherever people are confronted by evidence of abuse. At least experience and growing knowledge will contribute to local excellence, areas of light in the surrounding gloom.

The evidence, however, is already growing that the cost of not addressing these issues systemically and holistically may be far greater than investing the resources to do it properly. After the long hot summers of the early 1990's Luis Rojas Marcos, then head of public mental health services for New York City was asked by the City to undertake research on the causes of violence. He found that the causes of violence are not manifold but unitary. Like Bob Johnson, he found that the seeds of violence are planted in childhood, nurtured in adolescence, and bear their bitter fruits in adult life (Las Semillas de la Violencia, 1995).

Childhood trauma leads to the fragmentation of the growing self and immerses the young victim in a world of terror and pain which continues indefinitely after the original trauma has ended, if it ends. The patterns of avoidance and intrusion which result generate dangerous and destructive behaviour. Violence, self-harm, drug and alcohol abuse, mental health problems, physical health problems, relationship problems, employment problems, child care problems, educational problems, criminal behaviour problems, conduct disorders, personality disorders – and this is not the full list. Paedophilia is a particularly toxic traumatic stressor. Victims of organised child sexual abuse are liable to very severe suffering in the continuum of possible manifestations of post traumatic stress disorder.

We are already paying for the consequences of childhood trauma. We pay the financial cost of the many fragmented services which have to address themselves to different bits of the presenting problem. We pay the bills, and practitioners provide the services, knowing that they are being far less effective than they could be and that often they are actually contributing to making the problem worse as they feed into the fragmentation of the self. We pay the social cost of violence and disruption and drug abuse and crime. Now may be the time to change.

Chapter 11

Implications

putting the pieces together

What are the implications of the issues arising from the effects of paedophile abuse? Again, I can only offer suggestions into what must be a collective exercise in discernment and creativity or many interconnected group exercises, as we bring together our various areas of knowledge, understanding, and experience. Much of this work is already going on, I expect, but it does not appear to me that it is being integrated into anything resembling a holistic and systemic strategic response. Indeed, there is not yet any clear social or political will or mandate for such strategic thinking and planning.

The importance of collective working on this, in linked groups with feedback and interaction, cannot be overstated. We are dealing with areas in which there is a history of massive repression, avoidance and denial on the one hand, and falsehood and subversion on the other. We have all been part of that history, and our vision will be patchy and cloudy. There is some parallel with the women's movement here, and with developing awareness of racism and all forms of cultural oppression.

There are, as I see it, five areas in which we need to make progress and interconnect:

- Research

- Education and training

- Treatment for victims

- Structures of support

- Work with perpetrators

These are systemic and cyclical and in no order of priority, although it is clear that the first four listed are of direct relevance to this exploration of the effects on victims of paedophilia, whereas work with perpetrators is a huge field in its own right to which I cannot do justice here. It is mentioned to indicate that these fields must interconnect; victims and perpetrators should not be considered in isolation from one another.

It is important to keep steady in our view the links between these individually absorbing areas of work, and the links between our different agencies and professional disciplines as we make progress. If we keep the systemic nature of the work clear before us even while we become immersed in our own part of it, then all the results generated will feed into the slow and painstaking process of generating the social and political will for change.

Research
1. Victims
This will be a challenging area of research, for paedophilia is such a hidden field. My word processing programme has a show/hide button; press it and all the hidden fields which have been determining the way the characters relate to one another spring into view. Social research has no such easy answers, and the organised sexual abuse of children is a field which has been hidden from us by many layers of denial and subversion. Nevertheless the problem is beginning to declare itself, and research is needed to give as clear a picture as possible.

Primary victims, the children who have been exploited by paedophiles as sexual objects, and the adults who were so exploited as children, are largely hidden from us. We need research to understand more about the lives and experiences and needs of those who are already known to us.

It is also vital to begin to gain a thorough understanding of the many ways in which child sexual abuse may have an impact on us through the undeclared victims living out their fragmented lives among us. Enlightened doctors, drug and alcohol workers, prison staff, workers in agencies for people with special needs such as homelessness, relationship counsellors, social workers, police officers, and others whose work brings them into contact with people who cannot hold together the bits of their lives, will know that there is a theme of abuse running through these fractured lives.

It would be worth bringing this information together so that we could have a look at it. Bob Johnson and Luis Rojas Marcos both tell us that in their considerable professional experience most, perhaps all, extremely violent people have been victims of extreme abuse as children. That is a very strong statement for them to make. Of course there may be all the violent people they have not come across who had a childhood free of trauma, but that is the point we do not have the information to know.

We need to know the behavioural consequences in adult life of a range of childhood traumas, and in particular we need to gain information about the particularly hidden field of the effects of organised child sexual abuse. If, as I suspect, this group contains within it very high levels of disordered behaviour and physical and mental ill-health, the research will soon provide a strong case for the cost of an integrated strategic approach actually being a saving compared with the cost we currently pay for allowing victims to stay traumatized. Especially if we can show evidence of effectiveness in treatment.

Research is needed into treatment options for primary victims. It is vital to gather together some reliable information on what works. As noted earlier, this will not be exclusive research but will allow for the requirement for holistic responses to post traumatic stress disorder. A wide range of therapeutic options will need to be evaluated for their effectiveness, and it is vital that there is a built in recognition that different treatment works well for different victims at different stages of the disorder and at different stages of their lives. Victims of post traumatic stress disorder need an extensive range of possible therapeutic approaches to be available, from which a trusted assessor of needs can select appropriately. If we are ever to achieve this we need accurate information about what works for whom under what circumstances.

Secondary victims, those who live with the primary victims, present a truly uncharted field for research. It is vital for us to discover what happens to people who live with and care for the devastated and fragmented self left after the assaults of organised child sexual abuse. We need to know who they are, the full range – from families, through fostering families and residential child care workers, to partners and children of adult victims. Research should tell us in what ways the experiences of different groups are similar and in what ways they differ, and what therapeutic or reparative strategies are effective.

This will by no means be all pain and distress. Children who foster have taught me that if they are allowed to tell the story, it is true that many of them have suffered but many have also valued their life with children who have been victims. Their talk of having learned much, of feeling somehow privileged as well as victimised, of valuing the lessons in courage and dignity the sufferers have provided in the midst of the chaos, echoes the descriptions of transformation recorded by Tedeschi and Calhoun (1995). Such positive experiences, however, have too often been used to justify victimising one set of children in order to provide a family to look after another. We need some hard information in this field.

Tertiary victims, the professionals across a range of disciplines whose work exposes them to the toxic effects of paedophilia, are another group about whom we need solid facts. Such research will require a strong social and organisational mandate, for workers are bound by a host of issues around confidentiality and professional ethics. Yet it is vital that we begin to discover the information we will need to build up appropriate responses.

We cannot provide for the needs of children who have been victims of paedophilia in a setting in which the work of exposing the abuse and caring for the victims disables workers and carers. The powerful forces of repression, avoidance and denial will never be overcome until we can provide a reasonable standard of safety for workers in the field.

Safety in this context does not imply lack of risk; most of the professionals involved work in areas which include some hazards. Workers will accept dangerous work if they can see what the risks are within reasonable limits of predictability. It is this uncharted territory which is disabling, this exploration of fields which workers think are familiar until the ground begins to give beneath their feet and the assumptions which are the foundations of their professional competence are shattered.

Given the current total absence of information on this subject, researchers will have the distinct advantage of being able to design research which actually addresses the questions which need to be answered. Some of the other areas of research will be drawn from existing projects which were set up to answer other questions but from which useful information on this subject can be drawn, whereas in the field of tertiary victimization in paedophilia there is virgin and un-charted territory for the researcher.

In my line of work this is known as reframing, putting another perspective on the fact that here is a whole group of workers who have been demonstrating exposure to toxicity and whose struggles have not gained recognition. We also need to know more about those who are exposed to stressors but do not develop symptoms or become victims of post traumatic stress disorder. That is something we must learn in all areas of this field; not just the stressors but also the protectors need to be charted for the benefit of those who come after.

2. Perpetrators

This is sure to be a growing area for research since most perpetrators of organised and network child sexual abuse are not known to the rest of us. If we develop a more powerful social and political mandate for the work, then we will begin to gain a more accurate picture of who paedophiles are, what they do, and how we can help them to stop doing it.

Research will be needed at every step of the way to keep everybody clear about what is happening. In this field not all research will be of a purely academic nature. The research which has been and will be undertaken by reputable journalists and reporters in preparing articles and documentaries is of great importance in developing understanding of a subject in which the people who are part of the usual channels of investigation of crime are often working with one hand tied behind their backs.

There is a growing understanding of how to work effectively with young perpetrators of child sexual abuse. In view of the vast difference between the few victims young perpetrators have abused compared with the many victims of adult offenders, this is immensely valuable preventive as well as remedial work. It is to be hoped that the inexorable logic of doing this work early and well will continue to be demonstrated by regular research.

3. Treatment

In addition to studying the results of treatment strategies and interventions for each of the victim groups and for perpetrators, it will be important to draw out more broad-based conclusions about the therapeutic tools we need at our disposal if we are to make an integrated response to paedophilia. Individual treatment options need to be set in a strategic base which corresponds with existing, or newly created, service provision. To do that effectively we need information.

Education

1. Victims

All victims of post traumatic stress disorder need to learn about the condition which afflicts them. The teaching may take place through group training, individual coaching, written information, audio or video tapes, or within counselling sessions or some other therapeutic milieu.

Primary victims have, by definition, been victimized in childhood. It is much more difficult for them to gain a clear picture of their own injuries, since they have very little sense of themselves in any other state. Secondary and tertiary victims are usually adults with a life before post traumatic stress disorder. It is often easier for them to make comparisons with a previous state, and learning about the nature and extent of the injury they have suffered may be both quicker and more complete.

2. Workers

People who work in professional fields which may become involved in the area of paedophilia need to learn about this work. Once we have research evidence the information will be more readily available. In the meantime it is crucially important to learn from the experiences of those who have been involved in such work, and to provide a forum in which the teaching and learning can take place.

Training is recognised as a protector against becoming disabled by traumatic stress, but only when it has a reasonably high correlation with the events as they unfold. I know of no groups of workers whose prior training had prepared them for some of the most professionally destructive issues they confronted in this work. There is a synergy in the simultaneous assaults on such fundamental assumptions as trust (colleague involvement in paedophilia), competence (lack of ability to provide an adequate service), confidence (undermining by colleagues, managers or the media), safety (threats to self and family), and so on.

This cumulative effect, in which the whole is so much greater than the sum of the parts, needs to be understood and transmitted to workers in preparation for the work they may have to undertake. Here, as elsewhere in life, forewarned is forearmed. Workers also need the opportunity to learn about support strategies and resources which have worked in other more charted areas of work, and to rehearse the creation of appropriate strategies for themselves. There are workers out there, and in here with me as I summon them to memory, whose careers, or marriages, or health, could have been saved if they had been given the opportunity to understand and rehearse and prepare for the work they fell into. Good workers, who could have gone on doing good things for the children. And there are children out there whose lives could have been saved if we had known how to do it.

3. Agencies

There is quite a range of agencies involved in this work, and an even greater range of learning needs. When we add the repression, avoidance and denial of individuals in an organisation to institutionalised versions of the same phenomena we can find quite fantastic structures in place for not-learning. A colleague once spoke to me of living in interlaced but mutually invisible worlds, the world of the primary victims and those of the various service providers and of the rest of society. A haunting image.

Agencies need to discover at every level, from governing body to basic grade worker, the best information available on childhood trauma and on the effects of organised child sexual abuse on children, carers and workers in the field. They need opportunities to assimilate this information despite the countervailing forces of their own individual and shared patterns of denial, and the subversive misinformation which is likely to come from anyone within the organisation who is a paedophile.

4. Workers in related settings

There are many fields of social, welfare and health provision which are not established to deal with the effects of paedophilia and which do not generally become involved in investigations, but in which staff are regularly in contact with victims and have to deal with a range of behaviours which are the result of the unrecognised post traumatic stress disorder.

These would include drug and alcohol projects, therapy and counselling services, hostels of various types, prison services, hospitals, various mental health settings, doctors' surgeries, employment projects, housing agencies, and the Samaritans. Staff in these agencies generally either have training which gives no preparation for dealing with the behaviours of victims of post traumatic stress disorder, or their training has prepared them for the behaviours but has construed them in a different and inaccurate way, or they are volunteers with little relevant training at all. An integrated approach would ensure that workers in all these services had a good grounding in the nature and effects of childhood trauma, the effects of organised child sexual abuse, and the realities of secondary and tertiary victimization.

5. The rest of society

The necessary circularity of a systemic approach recognises that we can do nothing without a social mandate, and that we cannot gain that mandate without public education, which must link in to each stage of the new knowledge we acquire as we explore the territory.

Every possible route to informing and educating the public can be recruited to the service of the children who need us to speak on their behalf. And the public, in this context, includes policy makers and law makers, school governors and mental health commissioners, solicitors and housing aid workers – people who do have a direct impact on the lives of victims. And the rest are those whose primary contribution will be to become part of a ground swell of public opinion which finally says "Enough is enough, up with this we will not put" and discovers that we do have the resources to contain the abuses and treat the victims once we discover the collective will to do it.

Treatment

Developing a genuinely holistic and systemic approach to the treatment of post traumatic stress disorder in general and the effects of organised child sexual abuse in particular will change our ways of providing services.

The key seems to lie in being able to provide a wide range of therapeutic options which are all pointed in the direction of the one therapeutic outcome, the recovery from trauma. The agencies able to provide these interventions currently span a range of disciplines, and access from one to another is cumbersome and uncoordinated. The result, as we have noted, is that agency interventions may actively contribute to the fragmentation of the self.

There is a need to integrate the service offered across the presenting problems, and also across time. It should be recognised at the outset that the victim will have different therapeutic needs at different stages of the journey to recovery. At present people become serial users of services, with each new service access requiring a new referral process and assessment, usually partial and inaccurate. That is in addition to becoming, at times, users of several services at the same time, each of which has been accessed separately and made its own assessment, and which may be mutually ignorant of the others' involvement.

A young man who was in the care of a local authority as a young child after severe abuse was placed successively in three abusive institutions, as a teenager was suicidal, became involved in drug taking and violent crime, went to prison, became homeless, developed physical illnesses as a result of the drug use, and is currently waiting for a place in a detox centre to become available. There are active debates between two local authorities and the health service over who is responsible for funding which aspects of the minimal treatment he will receive for the most pressing of his disabling problems.

This is one story but it could be many, and is in reality repeated day by day in all our towns and cities. Those who know about these things are telling us that most people who develop these destructive behaviour patterns have suffered childhood trauma, and that broadly speaking those who have suffered the most trauma are the most disabled. And they have been invisible, an interpenetrating world living out their suffering among us and yet remaining invisible.

The problems have not been invisible. As a community we know that we have a problem with crime, and drug abuse, and violence. But the holistic understanding of what it is that happens to people when the injury of trauma fragments the core of them – that has been missing. We need to learn ways of providing services which are responsive to persons in the complexity of the responses they generate to post traumatic stress disorder and also responsive to the longitudinal course of the disorder. Services which have the flexibility across range and across time.

Treatment also should be readily accessible to primary, secondary, and tertiary victims as needed. It requires another set of creative thinking to resolve issues of equality of provision for each of the groups of people who may become victims of post traumatic stress disorder as a result of the effects of paedophilia. Once we have heard the voice of the silenced children, however, we will surely recognise that we cannot provide an adequate service for them if we do not take care of the carers and the workers who will supply the service.

Structures of support
Once the toxicity of this work is recognised, it becomes clear that we need very strong structures around it for people to do it safely. Carers and workers should have access to any combination of: individual peer support, group peer support, supervision, inter-agency support, external consultancy, counselling, therapy, agency and interagency consultancy, and debriefing.

'Grief leadership' is important (Ursano, Grieger and McCarroll in van der Kolk *et al*, 1996, p452), and agencies should take note that leaders will be needed who can sustain congruent affect in harrowing situations. They need to be able to maintain the focus on the task, while also sustaining contact with, and expressiveness about, the feelings of everyone involved, including their own feelings and those of their workers. These grief leaders will themselves have considerable support needs, as they will have a high exposure to toxic experiences.

Primary victims have exceptional needs for continuing support. Children who are looked after by the local authority will not cease to need this intensive support from trusted carers at the age of sixteen, seventeen, or eighteen. Child victims of post traumatic stress disorder invariably have need of trustworthy and reliable support well into adulthood, and children who have been victims of paedophile abuse may not begin to experience the relationship with their principal carers as trustworthy until after they have reached adult years. If that support is withdrawn at just the point when they could most have used it, they are bereft indeed.

Those who currently do provide this support are often doing so on a relatively informal basis. This is not an adequate response on the part of the rest of us. Victims are very demanding people, and the experience of being the supporter can be intensely draining. The work of carers and families in continuing to support the victim of paedophilia into adult life should be recognised and in its turn supported.

Work with perpetrators
This is primarily a consideration of the effects of paedophilia on victims. Nevertheless it is important to acknowledge the interface between this and work with perpetrators, especially investigative work. The fields are inextricably entangled, and investigating officers may also become tertiary victims.

It is to be hoped that the whole question of the uncovering of paedophile activity will also be organised nationally and internationally on a strategic basis. This strategic planning should take full account of the needs of victims. At present there is great pain at this juncture of linked but mutually damaging needs. Victims suffer terrible harm through being caught up in long and difficult attempts to bring criminals to an accounting. Even when the prosecutions go ahead and are successful the children or adults who were child victims are damaged by them. When they fail, and many currently do, then the damage can be horrifying.

Transformation

Can we transform ourselves, or open ourselves to the possibility of transformation? At the level of the organisations, agencies, and workers involved we can because we must. The work is ours to do. If we continue to do it with the half-hearted and ambivalent social and political mandate we have at present, then we must make the best we can of it. It should not be so very hard for us to find the will, for we are the ones who hear the voices of the children. If the will is there, then many creative possibilities can be explored, to make the best use of the systems and resources available to us.

Wholehearted transformation at the level of the social and political community in which we live may seem too large a hope. Yet we should take heart from the understanding that this is not a reasoned rejection of the plea for recognition. Where avoidance and denial are the forces at work, change can come swiftly and unexpectedly. We may be look-ing at the image and be able to see quite clearly what it is, a recognisable figure steady in our view, and then suddenly, in the blink of an eye, there is a shift of perspective; ground and figure shift, and what was previously invisible now becomes our common sense.

If the steady process of education and explanation were to bring us to that point, if suddenly the invisible victims became clear to the society in which they live and on which, like all of us, they depend, then the social and political will for change would follow.

After that it would be a question of money. I am reminded of an old Quaker story. The carter's horse died in mid-journey, a disaster for the carter and for the community he served. People from the village gathered round to commiserate. Everyone said how very sorry they were. Then one turned to another and said, "I'm sorry £5. How much is thee sorry, friend?"

This transformation can happen. I have a long memory. I can remember my great grandmother who died when I was two. Authentic infant memories of the texture and colour of skin and fabric and the smell of camphor and talc. She was the wife and daughter of miners, like me she was kin to those who had died. They press around me now, the children whose short lives were filled with coal dust and mud, with stifling darkness and water, the sweat of it and the stench.

I know that the society in which the mining communities lived did not see them; they were invisible, the children were invisible. Then people began to notice them. And gradually, bit by bit, a society emerged where it was not all right for children to work in the pits. Where eight years, or six years, or ten, were not considered enough of a childhood. The society developed a political will, and the children stopped dying.

Children who are victims of paedophilia are deprived of their childhood. Some of them have suffered harm which, very precisely, is worse for them than dying. They cannot stop being victims and become survivors unless we do something about it. Some transformations have to happen.

Bibliography

Angelou, M. (1995) *The Complete Collected Poems*, Virago

Angelou, M. (1984) *I Know Why the Caged Bird Sings*, Virago

Barker, P. (1992) *Regeneration*, Penguin

Barker, P. (1994) *The Eye in the Door*, Penguin

Barker, P. (1996) *The Ghost Road*, Penguin

Bateson, G. (1972) *Steps to an Ecology of Mind*, Ballantine Books

Bettelheim, B. (1991) *The Informed Heart*, Penguin

Bibby, P. (ed.) (1996) *Organised Abuse: The Current Debate*, Arena

Bowlby, J. (1991) *Attachment and Loss*, (three volumes: *Attachment, Separation,* and *Loss)*, Penguin

Bronfenbrenner, U. (1979) *The Ecology of Human Development*, Harvard University Press

Brown, D., Scheflin, A.W. and Hammond, D.C. (1998) *Memory, Trauma Treatment, and the Law*, Norton

Carter, R. (1998) *Mapping the Mind*, Weidenfeld and Nicolson

Chu, J.A. (1998) *Rebuilding Shattered Lives: the responsible treatment of post traumatic and dissociative disorders*, John Wiley

Coles, R. (1986) *The Moral Life of Children*, Houghton Mifflin

Fahlberg, V.I. (1994) *A Child's Journey through Placement*, British Agencies for Adoption and Fostering

Frankl, V. (1997) *Man's Search for Ultimate Meaning*, Insight

Goleman, D. (1996) *Emotional Intelligence*, Bloomsbury

Griffin, S. (1984) *Woman and Nature: the roaring inside her*, The Women's Press

Gross, R. (1996) *Psychology: the science of mind and behaviour*, Hodder and Stoughton

Hodgkinson, P.E. and Stewart, M. (1991) *Coping with Catastrophe: a handbook of post-disaster psychosocial aftercare*, Routledge

Hopkins, G.M. (1996) *Selected Poems*, Oxford University Press

Hunt, G. (ed.) (1998) *Whistleblowing in the Social Services: public accountability and professional practice*, Arnold

Janoff-Bulman, R. (1992) *Shattered Assumptions: towards a new psychology of trauma*, The Free Press

Joseph, S., Williams, R. and Yule, W. (1997) *Understanding Post-Traumatic Stress: a psychosocial perspective on PTSD and treatment*, John Wiley

169

Kinchin, D. (1998) *Post Traumatic Stress Disorder: the invisible injury*, Success Unlimited

Kismaric, C. and Heiferman, M. (1992) *Frida Kahlo: the camera seduced*, Chronicle Books

Laing, R.D. (1965) *The Divided Self*, Pelican

Lerner, H.G. (1990) *The Dance of Anger*, Pandora

Levi, P. (1960) *If This is a Man*, Orion Press

Lomax, E. (1996) *The Railway Man*, Vintage

MacNeice, L. (1966) *The Collected Poems*, Faber and Faber

Miller, A. (1990) *Thou Shalt Not Be Aware: society's betrayal of the child*, Pluto Press

Morrison, B. (1997) *As If*, Granta Publications

Parkinson, F. (1995) *Listening and Helping in the Workplace*, Souvenir Press

Parkinson, F. (1993) *Post-Trauma Stress*, Insight

Pirsig, R.M. (1993) *Lila: an Inquiry into Morals*, Black Swan

Reason, P. and Rowan, J. (1981) *Human Inquiry: a Sourcebook of New Paradigm Research*, John Wiley

Rojas Marcos, L. (1995) *Las Semillas de la Violencia*, Espasa Hoy

Scott, M.J. and Stradling, S.G. (1992) *Counselling for Post-Traumatic Stress Disorder*, Sage

Shotter, J. (1984) *Social Accountability and Selfhood*, Basil Blackwell

Stamm, B.H. (ed.) (1995) *Secondary Traumatic Stress: self-care issues for clinicians, researchers, and educators*, Sidran Press

Steiner, G. (1992) *After Babel: aspects of language and translation*, Oxford University Press

Stoppard, T. (1967) *Rosencrantz and Guildenstern are Dead*, Faber and Faber

Tavris, C. (1989) *Anger: the misunderstood emotion*, Touchstone

Tedeschi, R.G. and Calhoun, G.C. (1995) *Trauma and Transformation: growing in the aftermath of suffering*, Sage

Utting, W. (1997) *People Like Us: the report of the review of the safeguards for children living away from home*, DoH/Welsh Office

van der Kolk, B.A., McFarlane, A.C., and Weisaeth, L. (eds.) (1996) *Traumatic Stress: the effects of overwhelming experience on mind, body and society*, The Guilford Press

Weinberger, E. (1991) *Octavio Paz: the collected poems, 1957-1987*, Grafton Books

Wolin, S.J. and Wolin, S (1993) *The Resilient Self: how survivors of troubled families rise above adversity*, Villard Press

Wyatt, G.E. and Powell, G.J. (1988) *Lasting Effects of Child Sexual Abuse*, Sage

INDEX